Distinguishing the Difference Between Leadership Skills

and Management Skills in an Organization

by

Marva Loretta Young

ABSTRACT

For a long time, people have tried to delineate between leadership and management skills in the business environment. Is such differentiation really necessary or should the skills be intertwined? Management skills are attained through institutions and developed through work experience. Leadership skills are without a doubt inborn and what one needs is an opportunity to bring them out. These skills complement each other especially in the modern day economy and separation of the skills is impracticable. There was probably a time where the differentiation of the two sets of skills was possible. The management's job was to plan, organize and coordinate whereas a leader could provide the inspiration.

The late Peter Drucker; a management guru was the first to understand that leadership and management skills could not be differentiated. The reason for this discovery was because of the emergence of a worker with knowledge. With this kind of worker he argued that one could no longer manage people and the new task at hand would be to lead people.

Nowadays, people look up to their managers not only for the management skills of organization which were meant to bring out efficiency but to also define them for purpose; a leadership skill. As my research is set to point out, the separation of the two sets of skills is possible but should organizations make an attempt of doing so, if they want the perfect package in a person. Grace Murray Hopper simply put it this way, "you manage things; you lead people."

DEDICATION

I would like to thank my parents for their love and devotion over the years. You have

been a support for me through everything. To my mom who will always give you the

truth, even if it hurts.

I love you both.

To God be the Glory, I want to thank God for paving the way in my life and making

this opportunity possible.

TABLE OF CONTENTS

LIST OF TABLES

LIST OF FIGURES

CHAPTER 1: INTRODUCTION

This research is meant to determine whether a business organization needs to distinguish the difference between leadership and management skills. The topic is important because of the emerging school of thoughts favoring either of the skills and the long debate surrounding this topic.

Many articles have been written trying to differentiate leadership and management skills. There has not been a definite answer on both and there are as many answers as questions asked on the importance of either. A recent article on the Wall Street Journal by Alan Murray (2010) titled "Guide to Management" shows that leadership and management must go hand in hand. He said that even though they were not necessarily linked they complement each other.

Multiple writers have written articles that show what skills are superior to the others. In truth, trying to discredit either skills could be fatal to both skills, as Murray pointed out they should complement each other. In this research, the evidence presented will show whether organizations should distinguish between the two sets of skills and the impact of what such distinction will have on the organization.

Background

There are multiple definitions of leadership and from these definitions is where skills of leadership can be derived. Stoghill (1974, pp. 43–44) defines leadership as "an interaction between members or a group. Leadership occurs when one group member modifies the motivation or competencies of others in the group." Gibson, Ivancevich, and Donnelly (2000, p. 272) define leadership as "the process by which an individual influences others to accomplish desired goals without coercive influence." From these definitions, leadership involves influence. There is a further distinction of a leader in a formal and an informal setting." Formal leaders have authority over their followers in an organization by virtue of their position whereas informal leaders exercise influence over followers by skills or friendship" (George & Gareth, 2005 pp. 357, 398).

A manager on the other hand gets things done through other people. A manager plans, delegates, assigns, disciplines, delegates in an organization among other functions. A manager need not have the influence from the understanding attained from the leadership definition. A manager exercises authority by virtue of being in the management position. A manager concentrates on the output of the workers and so the management relationship with them is that of efficiency.

From a business organization's context, the concern is on the management or a formal leader. The need is to ask this question in the context of distinguishing the two sets of skills, who is a manager without leadership skills? This could be the 'old-school' kind of manager who has no concern over what the process of the output is so long as the output is there to be seen. This is undesirable in the modern day economy whereby organizations are searching for, first the manager with good qualifications and going the extra step of searching for a manager with strong leadership attributes. The ideal manager should possess leadership skills. Part of the reason leadership skills have become so important is the competitive nature of the modern business world. Many companies are 'over-managed' and 'under-led' and need to develop their capacity to exercise leadership (Bertocci, 2009).

Management skills are imparted on formally through institutions and thereafter developed through experience. The process of attaining leadership skills is quite divisive. Some believe leaders are born while others believe they are made.

There exist differences between leaders and managers. An example is in this case where leaders' followers are free to follow the leader; while in the case of managers employees lack the freedom to do so. If an employee fails to follow the manager, there is the risk of losing the job. John Kotter (2009) in his article "What Leaders Really Do" states that one of the primary differences between management and leadership is on the basic functions. Whereas management is on complexity on organizational issues, leadership is about vision and change and is centered on the future.

Leadership and management is a set of different skills. The best leaders are not necessary the best managers and vice versa. What a leader possesses a manager may lack. A leader's understanding of a discipline may be at another level and may need somebody with the management skills to execute it. In the real world it is hard to find a person coupled with both leadership and management skills. Most organizations have leaders whose task is different and hire people with management skills. A good example is Facebook when they hired Sheryl Sandberg.

The strength of qualitative research is its ability to provide complex textual descriptions of how people experience a given research issue. It provides information about the human side of an issue that is often contradictory behaviors, beliefs, opinions, emotions, and relationships of individuals. Qualitative methods are also effective in identifying intangible factors, such as social norms, socioeconomic status, gender roles, ethnicity, and religion, whose role in the research issue may not be readily apparent (Cooper & Schindler, 2014).

Managers basically do business research to understand how and why things happen. If the manager needs to know only what happened, or how often things happened, quantitative research methodologies would serve the purpose. But to understand the different meanings that people place on their experiences often requires qualitative research techniques that delve more deeply into people's hidden interpretations, understandings, and motivations. Qualitative research is designed to tell the researcher how (process) and why (meaning) things happen as they do (Cooper & Schindler, 2014).

Problem Statement

A leaderless organization is like an army without generals. Work forces need the leadership of skilled and experienced individuals to provide guidance and a single direction for all employees to follow. Leaders are invaluable when it comes to formulating and communicating new strategic directions, and communicating with and motivating employees to increase dedication to organizational goals (Ingram, 2014).

Leadership acts as the catalyst that makes all other elements work together; without leadership, all other business resources lie dormant. Savvy business leaders are in tune with the needs and issues of their subordinates, and keep up-to-date with new developments in leadership theory and methodology to maximize their effectiveness (Ingram, 2014).

According to Ingram (2014), business leaders serve a range of important functions in their organizations. Leaders are responsible for training employees to perform their tasks effectively, as well as for supervising the actual completion of those tasks on a regular basis. Leaders must inspire employees to get excited about the company and their work, pushing them to excel and helping them along the way. Leaders are also tasked with protecting the employees under their supervision from internal and external threats, including everything from political backstabbing to physical security (Ingram, 2014).

Different leaders employ different leadership styles. Leaders with a command and control style formulate ideas on their own and dictate actions to their employees. Collaborative leaders come up with ideas with the assistance of employees from all levels of the organization, leveraging employees' creativity to boost company performance. Facilitative leaders delegate almost all productive tasks to subordinates, and focus on providing their employees with everything they need to excel in their jobs. Business owners' leadership styles are extremely important in crafting company culture (Ingram, 2014).

Purpose of the Study

The purpose of this study is to show that management and leadership are not the same thing. The two are related, but their central functions are different. Managers provide leadership, and leaders perform management functions. But managers do not perform the unique functions of leaders. The public sector develops a lot of good managers, but very few leaders. Government focuses too much on abstract or formal education, rather than experience. Developing managers and leaders involves stages of understanding, not prescriptively, but conceptually. Becoming a leader requires understanding oneself. There are many tools available to help with that assessment. Today the federal system, both its structure and processes, is changing. Civil servants are going to a new place, and it will take leaders (not just managers) to get them there (Colvard, 2003).

Researchers have said there are some very real, fundamental differences between leaders and managers, which form an enormous gulf, separating leaders from managers. Management is not a training ground for true leadership. That is one of the real dilemmas facing businesses today. It is critical to have both leaders and managers to drive a business forward. It is also vital to know the differences between the two. Leaders are adept at influencing and directing others, skillful at building relationships and masterful at solving problems and making decisions. Meanwhile, managers succeed by working within established guidelines (Sweeney, 2001).

If the population of the people are less than 300, for instance, it may be possible to survey the entire population, rather than choose a sample. When it is not possible to survey everybody the researcher will need to select a sample. Results from the people in the sample gives an estimate of what the results would have been had the whole population been surveyed. There are several different ways to identify the sample and the approach chosen will depend upon the purpose of the evaluation, and the size of the evaluation budget. The first question to ask is whether one wants a random or a non-random sample (Cooper & Schindler, 2014).

The population, or target population is any complete, or the theoretically specified aggregation of study elements. It is usually the ideal population or universe to which research results are to be generalized. It had been noted that "because many populations of interest are too large to work with directly, techniques of statistical sampling have been devised to obtain samples taken from larger populations" (Proctor, 2003, p.100).

Significance of the Study

This research will help define the need for the leadership of skilled and experienced individuals to provide guidance and a single direction for all employees to follow. Leaders are invaluable when it comes to formulating and communicating new strategic directions, as well as communicating with and motivating employees to increase dedication to organizational goals.

There are several differences between leaders and managers. A manager is an individual who has received a title or position that allows him or her the right to direct and control the behavior of others in their department. Leadership is more about interpersonal relationships and it involves inspiring, motivating, influencing and changing the behaviors of others in the pursuit of a common goal. Whereas leaders embrace change; managers tend to uphold the status quo. Leaders aim for effectiveness, and; managers' efficiency (Cooper & Schindler, 2014).

There are several differences that will be used to analyze the distinctions between managers and leaders while forming a corporate strategy. These distinctions fall under the concerns of creation of purpose, developing a network for achieving the agenda, execution, outcomes and focus timeframe. The contrast between leaders and managers will be shown during each stage (Cooper & Schindler, 2014).

During the creation of purpose managers tend to focus on budgets, create steps and look for resources to support those goals. Leaders on the other hand establish direction and create a vision and develop strategies needed to reach those visions. When one thinks of creating a vision Steve Jobs comes to mind; he had a vision of Apples success and he took the company to greater heights by introducing the iPhone, iPod and iPad (2011).

Managers, while developing a network for achieving the agenda get the staff together, create structure for achieving plans, delegate responsibility and authority develop procedures and create monitoring systems. Leaders set up people so they are aligned with the target, communicate with those whose cooperation is needed and create team groups that share and buy into the team's vision. Examples of a company's vision are linked to its vision statement; such as Toyota's vision statement *"To become the most successful and respected lift Truck Company in the U.S."* Any team that is put together must buy into the company's vision in order to succeed (Toyota's Vision and Mission Statement, 2015).

During the execution stage, managers control and solve problems while monitoring results and giving corrective action. Leaders tend to motivate and influence while helping people solve roadblocks in the project and helping them to show personal initiative.

During the outcomes stage, managers become very predictable and try to maintain the status quo. Leaders want change and challenge the status quo of the group. Whereas managers are not willing to go outside the box and they try to keep things the same; leaders will embrace change and challenge the team to think outside the box (Cooper & Schindler, 2014).

The focus timeframe has the manager having efficiency of operations in the short term and trying to avoid potential risk, maintaining and imitating. Leaders outcomes are long-term and takes risk while innovating and originating.

Leaders must recognize that managerial duties are also important. Managers have difficulty recognizing the interpersonal nature involved with leadership. Most research says that leadership can be taught and learned. Although management duties come along with the title the acts of leadership can be taught throughout an organization (Richards, 2014).

Leaders and leadership styles may need to be changed to suit specific situations. A new CEO in an established company, for example, may benefit from altering his or her leadership style to be more in line with the culture of his or her new company. Top executives themselves may need to be switched out from time to time if a company's performance establishes a pattern of decline (Richards, 2014).

The best leaders do not attempt to take advantage of employees and are always ensuring that their business practices follow the most acceptable social standards and norms. With so many workers under them in a big business, imparting a strong sense of ethics will ensure their workers maintain the company's integrity (Richards, 2014).

According to Richards (2014), effective business leadership is critical for meeting employee, customer and business needs. Leadership skills are skills that can, fortunately, be learned. It is not true that leaders are born, not made. Business leadership skills generally center on the ability to communicate effectively, the ability to focus on the big picture, and the ability to gather and analyze information. Leadership skills in business are developed over time. By consistently applying their leadership principles, leaders will begin to have dramatic effects on their organization.

Nature of the Study

For this study, qualitative data will be used and it is not important to have a sample that statistically represents the whole population. Qualitative research is interested in gaining greater detailed description and explanation, from fewer participants. A random sample is, therefore, not needed. However, the researcher still wants some connection between the people in the sample and the wider population of interest, so that they can transfer the findings beyond just the people in the sample. Samples for qualitative research methods are usually smaller than for quantitative research. Although the researcher cannot generalize the findings as well as in a random sample, it is normally easier, quicker, and cheaper to use non-random sampling (Cooper & Schindler, 2014).

Decisions about sample size depend on whether the data is quantitative or qualitative. For qualitative data, it is customary to use a method called *'theoretical saturation'* (Glaser & Strauss, 1967). This means that sampling continues until no new theories are emerging from the data collected. When the data stops revealing new information on the issues the researcher are interested in, it is called the saturation point, the sampling can stop. For quantitative data, statistical calculations will be used to determine how large the sample should be. These calculations are discussed in the Scope section. For this study qualitative data research will be used.

Research Questions

1. Is there a significant relationship between leadership skills and an organization achieving effective, overall corporate strategy?

2. Is there a significant relationship between management skills and an organization achieving effective, overall corporate strategy?

3. Do organizations need to distinguish the difference between leadership skills and management skills?

This study will assess the leadership ability of managers, based on participant responses. Employees will be asked to rate the leadership ability of their managers using an ordinal Likert scoring system, where a score of *strongly agree, agree, neutral, disagree or strongly disagree* indicates leadership characteristics displayed by the manager. To establish a foundation for the study, survey questions have been developed that will be proven or disproven throughout the process. The Likert scale implemented determines the rate of leadership skills and the components stem from participant response, specifically the quality of a manager's leadership ability within the work environment (Wilcox, 2012).

One of the challenges with testing through survey is rationalizing the truth (Poletiek, 2013). That is, the researcher must assess whether an employee (who rated the manager extremely low) is responding to a workplace incident or if he or she truly believes that the manager does not demonstrate leadership ability in the work environment. With a smaller sample size, the likelihood of a respondent providing an extreme response in an untruthful manner is reduced. Still, these extreme responses must be indicated by the researcher as outliers and not be applied to the study as valid data (Poletiek, 2013).

Implementation of inferential statistics within this study requires the researcher to differentiate between two groups. That is, one group believes that the manager demonstrates leadership skills in the work environment, indicated with a rating above *"neutral."* The second group does not believe that the manager represents a leader, indicated by a rating below *"neutral."* Because it is not feasible or likely possible to examine the entire population individually, a sample size will be used for this study. A sample size of 160 employees is significant for this study. A confidence interval is used as a tool to measure statistical data based on the responses collected from the sample size of 160 employees (Wilcox, 2012).

The study will use qualitative data to fully assess the research questions and eventually prove or disprove the research based on the findings. Confidence intervals enhance the mean, which is a significant descriptive statistic in order to broaden the study, instead of limiting the study to a small sample size which may have no impact on the population as a whole. Further, confidence intervals create an opportunity for future research in this area. The straight-forward nature of the research questions that have been developed ensure minimal confusion in proving or disproving them through the use of data collection and the development of descriptive statistics (Wilcox, 2012).

Survey Questions

1. How effective is the training you receive from your supervisor?

2. How available to employees is your supervisor?

3. How approachable is your supervisor?

4. How improved is your performance after getting feedback from your supervisor about your work?

5. How often does your supervisor give you feedback about your work?

The supervisors at an organization are only as good as how well they manage their employees and want to make sure they're getting the job done right. These questions will help to determine if the organization's managers are effective. These questions will find out from employees how reasonable they think their managers are and where they see room for improvement.

Interview Questions

1. How have you influenced employees to follow your strategic vision for the organization?

2. What are the most important values and ethics you demonstrate as a leader? Give us an example of these in practice.

3. Name some situations in which a leader may fail. Tell us about a time when you failed as a leader?

4. What role does leadership play for a manager? How have you demonstrated this with your managers?

5. What methods have you used to gain commitment from your team?

Leadership interview questions focus on exploring and evaluating recognized leadership competencies. The questions are designed to assess whether the candidate has both leadership skills and leadership potential. Leadership interview questions will require candidates to provide examples of how they have demonstrated these leadership competencies and are asked in the format of behavioral or competency based interview questions.

Conceptual Framework

Over the years there have been several views of how leadership and management are different. Abraham Zaleznik (1977) gave us several views on how managers and leaders differ. Zaleznik saw leaders as inspiring visionaries concerned with substance; whereas, managers he viewed as planners who have concerns with process. He drew 12 distinctions between the two groups:

- Managers administer; leaders innovate.

- Managers ask how and when; leaders ask what and why.

- Managers focus on systems; leaders focus on people.

- Managers do things right; leaders do the right things.

- Managers maintain; leaders develop.

- Managers rely on control; leaders inspire trust.

- Managers have short-term perspective; leaders have long-term perspective.

- Managers accept the status-quo; leaders challenge the status-quo.

- Managers have an eye on the bottom line; leaders have an eye on the horizon.

- Managers imitate; leaders originate.

- Managers emulate the classic good soldier; leaders are their own person.

- Managers copy; leaders show originality.

Zalenik (1977) also provided us the exact difference between the role of managers and leaders:

- The best word for managers is balance; the best word for leaders is change.

- Managers want to smooth things out; leaders want to shake things up.

- Managers think about how to oversee the existing order of things; leaders think about how to shape the future.

- Managers think about execution; leaders go for ideas.

- Managers seek control; leaders seek out risk.

- Managers seek stability and, therefore, prefer to act quickly to solve problems; leaders handle ambiguity well and can delay closure.

- Managers focus on problem-solving and achieving the results to which the organization is committed; leaders incite people to think about what could be.

- Managers view work as a process of compromises so that everyone can be a winner; leaders look for opportunities for large gains at the risk of failure.

- Managers tend to be social but not as emotionally involved; leaders have high emotional intelligence and empathy.

- Managers send "signals"; leaders send "messages."

- Managers focus on following the correct procedures to resolve an issue (the process); leaders focus on the substance of an issue.

John Kotter (1996) thought managers are more involved with planning and developing, organizing, staffing, controlling and problem solving; whereas leaders establish direction, align people in the right positions and motivate and inspire people to overcome barriers to satisfy basic human needs. For most of this century, there were thousands and thousands of large organizations for the first time in human history, the organizations did not have enough good managers to keep all those bureaucracies functioning. So many companies and universities developed management programs, and hundreds of thousands of people were encouraged to learn management on the job. And they did. But people were taught little about leadership. To some degree, management was emphasized because it's easier to teach than leadership. But even more so, management was the main item on the 20th century agenda because that was what was needed. For every entrepreneur or business builder who was a leader, hundreds of managers are needed to run their ever-growing enterprises (Kotter, 1996). Unfortunately, in the world today, this emphasis on management has often been institutionalized in corporate cultures that discourage employees from learning how to lead. This research will examine the effects of management and leadership on the organizational structure.

Definition of Terms

Administrator. A person responsible for running a business, organization etc. (Oxford University Press, 2016)

Administration. The process or activity of running a business, organization etc., the action of giving, dispensing or applying something. (Oxford University Press, 2016)

Leaders. A person who leads or commands a group, organization or country. (Oxford University Press, 2016)

Leadership styles. The manner and approach of providing direction, implementing plans, and motivating people. As seen by employees, it includes the total pattern of explicit and implicit actions performed by their leader. The first major study of leadership styles was performed in 1939 by Kurt Lewin who led a group of researchers to identify different styles of leadership (Lewin, Lippit, & White, 1939). This early study has remained quite influential as it established the three major leadership styles: *Authoritarian or autocratic.* The leader tells his or her employees what to do and how to do it, without getting their advice (Lewin, Lippit, & White, 1939); *Participative or democratic.* The leader includes one or more employees in the decision making process, but the leader normally maintains the final decision making authority (Lewin, Lippit, & White, 1939); *Laissez-fair (free-rein).* The leader allows the employees to make the decisions, however, the leader is still responsible for the decisions that are made (Lewin, Lippit, & White, 1939)

Managers. A person responsible for controlling or administering all or part of a company or similar organization. (Weyer, 2011)

Management. A mufti-purpose organ that manages business and manages managers and manages workers and work. (Drucker, 2007)

Organizational structure. The hierarchy of authority in an organization and determine how the information level flows among management. The structure depends on the organizations objectives and strategies. (Pugh, 1990)

Skills. The ability to do something well. Expertise. (Weyer, 2011)

Assumptions

Assumptions in a test are things that could be out of the control of the researcher but if they weren't there the study would be irrelevant. While conducting a survey, the assumption is that the respondents will answer truthfully. When conducting a survey, the assumption is that the sample is representative of the population the researcher wishes to make reference to. Leedy and Ormrod (2010) states, "Assumptions are so basic that, without them, the research problem itself could not exist" (p. 62).

- The assumption is that organizations will look at the entire skill set of an upper level manager before they hire them to run the business.

- The assumption is that during the surveys, employees will be honest about their supervisors' leadership/management skills.

- The assumption is that the sample population chosen will understand the scope of the question asked and respond accordingly.

Scope, Limitations and Delimitations

The limitations could deal with the number of subjects questioned, the research will need a worthy population to get a valid outcome. Another issue is if the answers of the participants taking the surveys can be trusted. Some subordinates might be afraid to give an honest opinion about their bosses because they are afraid of retaliation.

The delimitations are that in order to control the population pool the right amount of participants must be decided ahead of time and the organizations that will be the test companies must be determined. Employees that have disciplinary problems in any organization, will be eliminated from the test, and employees employed less than 60 days will not be chosen to participate in the test pool.

There are various free-to-use sample size calculators available on the internet. When using a sample size calculator, enter a 5% margin of error and a 95% confidence level as defaults. Enter the size of the total population, for example, suppose there are 10,000 older residents in the locality, and the tool will calculate the minimum number of people in the sample. To have strong statistical findings it is also advisable to speak to a statistics expert about sample size. Generally speaking the larger the sample size, the more reliable the findings. However, there is no benefit in going beyond a maximum of about 1,500 people in a sample (Cooper & Schindler, 2014).

Summary

In this research qualitative testing method will be used to decide the outcome of the hypothesis and survey questions. The research will determine the sample population used and decide which organizations will be used to apply the test. During Chapter 2 the literary review, several literary papers will be reviewed that will support the research theory. This chapter will lead to the next phase in completing the dissertation process.

CHAPTER 2: LITERATURE REVIEW

The following literature review provides a foundation of the proposed study by providing an outline of the difference in leadership and management skills as it relates to organizational success. The review details an analysis and examination of the characteristics of leadership and management skills as noted by several different scholars. This analysis is followed with a discussion of several different theories of leadership and management. The research completes an analysis of leadership and management, and closes with an analysis of in relation to successful organizational outcomes.

Literature Review

Leadership and management are not two mutually exclusive terms and have many similarities. They seem to differ in a number of respects though they are qualities that go hand in hand. Mangers are often mistakenly talked about as leaders whereas in reality there is a great difference between leadership and management. The biggest difference between leadership and management arises from the way they motivate people who work around them, as this sets the tone for all other aspects of an organization. Management usually has an aura or authority vested in it by the company. Subordinates work under it, and largely do as they are told. This is a transactional style in which managers tell workers what to do and workers comply because they are promised a reward (salary or bonus). Management is normally paid to get things done within the constraints of time and money. Management tends to come from stable backgrounds and lead relatively comfortable lives. This makes them averse to taking risks and they seek to avoid conflict as much as possible. In terms of people, they like to run a happy ship (Seabury, 2014).

Leaders on the other hand do not have subordinates. They tend to have followers, and following is more of a voluntary activity than a forced one as in the case of subordinates. Leadership is a charismatic, transformational style. Leaders do not tell people what to do as this does not inspire them. Leadership appeals to workers and they desire to follow the leaders. Leadership can make workers walk into dangers and situations they normally would not consider risking. Leadership requires giving credit to people and motivating them by praising them for their good work. Leadership requires taking all the blame and shielding the followers in sharp contrast to management which is always happy to pass the buck on to the subordinates and is the first to take credit for good performance. Although both leadership and management are work focused and strive for better results, leadership motivates and encourages workers whereas management treats them as mere resources. Whereas management is averse to risk, leadership is risk seeking. Leadership happily breaks rules to get things done whereas management tends to follow the rules and regulations (Seabury, 2014).

American author and scholar, Warren Bennisin his 1989 book "On Becoming a Leader," listed the differences between a manager and a leader. The list is as follows:

- The manager administers; the leader innovates.
- The manager is a copy; the leader is an original.
- The manager maintains; the leader develops.
- The manager focuses on systems and structure; the leader focuses on people.
- The manager relies on control; the leader inspires trust.
- The manager has a short-range view; the leader has a long-range perspective.
- The manager asks how and when; the leader asks what and why.

- The manager has his or her eye always on the bottom line; the leader's eye is on the horizon.
- The manager imitates; the leader originates.
- The manager accepts the status quo; the leader challenges it.
- The manager is the classic good soldier; the leader is his or her own person.
- The manager does things right; the leader does the right thing.

Leadership is putting others before yourself and entails articulating a vision of something larger than the individuals involved. Leadership is helping those involved understand their role in achieving it and inspiring them to take on seemingly insurmountable challenges because they believe in the vision to the core of their being. Leadership and management work hand in hand but truly are fundamentally different concepts (Lopez, 2014).

Lopez (2014) emphasized that leadership and management are based on the use of an instructional approach. Leadership in this article is seen as visionary, and able to influence and motivate others. Managers are characterized as bureaucrats whose function is to plan, budget, control, and organize. Frederick Taylor, in the 1900s, emphasized that management theories are usually tied to scientific management. The article used the steel and railroad business as an example of why scientific management received widespread publicity after 1910. Scientific management was sought after by companies that looked to increase their productivity (Lopez, 2014).

This study addressed the idea that business students are not receiving appropriate business instructions based on the education they are receiving in the 21st century.

Business students would find it more glamorous to become a leader than a manager based on the different concepts of the two in the educational instructions today (Lopez, 2014).

The hypothesis is based on (a) the notion that if leadership is more significant than management, then there is no interest in learning management skills (b) remediating the idea that management is regarded as mediocre when compared to leadership (Lopez, 2014). If management and leadership are taught as one business course, then business students would have a definite business foundation. Management and leadership are described, compared and contrasted; and instructional biases are presented in order to specify the reasoning for why writers think leaders are better than managers (Lopez, 2014).

Several authors have their own theory on leadership and management. Northouse (2009) saw leadership as a trait, an ability, a skill, and a behavior. Johnson (2009) focused on transformational leadership; he saw it as idealized influence, inspirational motivation, intellectual stimulation and individualized consideration. Potts (2001) saw emotional intelligence as more important than intelligence alone and noted that emotional intelligence consist of self-awareness, self-management, social awareness and relationship management. Potts (2001) saw leaders as more important than managers, mainly because of their ethical behavior. He saw management as having no defining morals of ethical dimension, they only serve the interest of the individual groups. The only concern of management is survival. Potts (2001) idea is that if ethics is taken out of leadership, what is left of management? This ideas is ingrained in scientific management. The conclusion is that based on the information from scholars, the authors felt management and leadership are complementary activities and should be taught as such (Lopez, 2014).

Mitut (2011) referred to leadership as interpersonal relationships based on: encouragement of sincerity, appreciation of initiatives, and proof of availability to subordinates, lack of favoritism, and representation of subordinates and stimulation of fair competition. The article showed that, in modern organizations, from nation-to-nation and from organization-to organization, there are indicators relating to time management, work-life balance, professional training, job satisfaction and job security that vary (Mitut, 2011).

In current organizations, with the changes in technological learning and elimination of communication barriers, organizations need leadership to be extremely efficient, competitive, and effective. When an organization has a lack of leadership, it is vulnerable and lacks insight into crisis situations, risking loss of control over human resources. There could also be a loss of competitiveness and loss of effective employees, which could lead to organizational failure (Mitut, 2011). Mitut (2011) concluded that managers which understands the role of organizational leadership, who practices empathy towards employees, controls their impulses and knows when to exert their authority, can create a calm situation for their subordinates, even in organizational crises.

Weathersby (1999) insisted that as brainpower has taken over as brawn in the workplace, a new understanding has taken place between companies and their employees, making it harder for managers competing for talent. Lifetime employment has decreased whereas workplace mobility has increased making turnover a management nightmare. Turnover at the management level is at an all-time high (Weathersby 1999).

Cornell University's Center for Advanced Human Resource Studies noted that the average executive changes companies three times during his or her working career. Career Mosiac and The Monster Board have created a broad, free market for upper level management that could result in project-by-project employment, instead of permanent employment in an organization. These changes could force managers to do their job differently, causing them to adopt a new approach to their jobs (Weathersby 1999).

The article contended that management is about controlling; the setting of priorities, the design of work and the achievement of results. By contrast, leadership is creating a common vision and getting subordinates to buy into that vision, which will create a high level of productivity. Leaders will need to control their emotions and the emotions of others working with them. For managers to recruit, motivate, and retain employees, customers, investors and shareholders have a "new" vision of the decision making process. The management model of tomorrow will focus on the process and the team, as well as on the individual's capability and performance (Weathersby 1999).

The article, leadership vs management. What's the difference? Discusses the pros and cons of networking in the health care management. The article had several suggestions for learning how to network; since 5% to 25% of jobs are advertised-networking allows one to tap into 75% of "hidden" jobs, joining professional organizations can help build contacts, volunteer with organizations in the community, carry copies of resumes and business cards around to help increase contacts, don't be afraid to ask for help, send thank you notes to contacts that have helped along the way and keep networking options open after finding a job; one never knows when they will need those contacts again.

The article stressed that for an organization to be successful it must have both capable managers and inspiring leaders. There are characteristics that managers and leaders have; leaders are labeled as being visionaries, collaborators, salespeople and negotiators. Managers are known for being captains, analysist, conductors and controllers. In the distinction between leadership and management, Wiesner (1997) felt one cannot be successful in today's business world unless they have a little of both (leadership and management). Wiesner (1997) discussed the difference between and characteristics of both. A leader is needed instead of a manager when making important operational business decisions. A manager is needed when one has to run a large, established, multi-divisional company. Managers are also used to maintain and improve the performance of a good team. Some people are capable of both and can be a manager and a leader (Wiesner, 1997).

The essential difference between leadership and management is that; resources are managed and people are led. In order to manage, one must organize, direct, and evaluate feedback. Then he or she must reorganize, redirect, and reevaluate until the business runs smoothly. Managers must also know their territory. In order to lead, one must understand, challenge, inspire and reward. Leaders inspire and challenge individuals and groups to accomplish things they thought impossible. A good leader shares everything with their subordinates; glory, money and future challenges (Wiesner, 1997).

Wiesner (1997) suggested that one can train managers but leadership qualities must be mined and refined. Everyone has the capacity to lead, they cannot be trained to that end but they can be led to discover out innate strengths. Leadership skills can be improved but not to the extent that management skills can be grown and taught.

Leadership is considered more of an art than a science. Management skills reside in the intellect. Leadership exist against a background of sensitivity to relationships, the ability to challenge and inspire, and an understanding of what people want in return for their inspired behavior (Wiesner, 1997).

Richardson (2007) argued the inconsistent with Cartesian and Newtonian dynamics, which the constellations of behavior recognized as leadership and management emerged from, and are sustained by, a dynamical, interdependent, and complex autopoietic system consistent with the demands of biological evolution. This study will develop leaders and managers as archetypal, representing archetypes as specific bundles of behavior. These archetypes, leadership and management, will be examined as representative of behavioral environmental adaptations that emerged as a result of the co-evolutionary relationship that subsumes the biological system and the environment. As archetypes, leadership and management, will be developed as resulting from genetics rather than environmental influence. The study will argue further, consistent with the dictates of the new emerging quantum science that the system supporting leadership and management emerged from, and is representative of, a greater physical system that subsumes all things, the animate and the inanimate, in a web of interdependence. The evidence that a hidden order is at work involving both physics and biology will be examined from the perspective of the leadership and management archetype (Richardson, 2007).

The research concluded that both leadership and management represent evolutionary archetypes, that they are interdependent, are embedded in the genetic system, and, working in tandem to comprise an autopoietic system, a system that mirrors the influence of the greater physical system in a self-similar, biofractal fashion. The research will rely on well accepted and emerging theories in quantum physics, biology, physical science, cultural anthropology, and psychology to support its conclusions (Richardson, 2007).

Sutton (2006) presented, in his study, two purposes for researching the differences between management and leadership. The first purpose is to examine the effectiveness of institutional leadership as compared to managerial leadership at the organizational level. Institutional models (transformation and conservator) and the managerial model (transactional) were used in the study to support the research and to manage any reform efforts that take place in organizations. Sutton examined the effectiveness of the models by observing the job satisfaction of employees who work under supervisors that utilize these models. The second purpose of the research was to investigate the impact of leadership styles on job satisfaction within the public sector (Sutton, 2006). The research was conducted in the Cuyahoga County Department of Children and Family Services, where the DCFS has structured reform programs that have been in effect for more than 10 years. The researcher used questionnaires, of the leadership staff members, categorizing leadership styles based on the three models. The research used self-administered job satisfaction surveys on employees to judge leadership styles. The conclusions of the research was as follows: there was an association between leadership styles and job satisfaction, institutional methods can be successfully employed at the managerial level, and the staff of institutional leadership models have higher job satisfaction than the staff of transactional leaders (as measured by overall mean scores) (Sutton, 2006).

Edward's (2000) research dealt with the pursuit of an understanding of the leadership behaviors in the West, particularly in the United States. Leadership behavior theories often reflect, themes, frameworks and paradigms in First World coinage. Leadership theory extended into government, corporate and civic settings in other parts of the world; although it is located in the Western world. Due to globalization, technological trends and information linkage created links to extend the boundaries of leadership skills and their theoretical definitions. Studying leadership qualities in multi-cultural settings under different geo-political situations gave insight into the mindset of Western civilization, which led towards a global conversation about leadership issues (Edwards, 2000).

The research examined issues in the distinction between leadership and management in the Western hemisphere, to test the elements of this difference of leadership and management practices in the country of Trinidad and Tobago in the; West Indies. The study placed emphasis on observing the specific concept of leadership/ management self-awareness. The assumptions used during the research were as follows: The difference between leaders (transformational) and managers (transactional) is a universal phenomenon, leaders and managers are not a theoretical abstraction; but is an everyday behavior as they interact with others, leadership is essential for national/societal development and, therefore, directly related to educational restructuring and schools are perfect sites for building the research behind leadership skills (Edwards, 2000).

Parisian (2009) researched how failed information technology projects continues while the experience of the user and organization gets broader. Managers and users should be trained properly to use the technology. Researchers must look at what is preventing the implementation of IT from being successful. This research focused of the internal and external reaction, to IT, of the user and the training that managers need to become change leaders. Parisian also addressed user needs and resistance to IT.

Several different literary reviews were covered to give credibility to the use of IT in the organization. Training presentations, including a PowerPoint, were developed, which entailed the topics of; theories of user attitudes and behavior, theories of user resistance and acceptance, how users cope with change, technology readiness, self-efficacy, change management and strategies for managing change. The use of pre-course assessment aided managers in getting into the correct frame of mind prior to the start of the training content and in identifying the gaps in the change management knowledge. The post course assessment tested manager's understanding of the training content and stressed the topic areas of importance that will assist in their next IT change project. The conclusion of the report ends with strategies that would help the manager with specific presentations, actions and responses they can do to improving acceptance and reducing resistance to information (Parisian, 2009).

Ever since the first publication on leadership, there has been an ongoing debate about the relevance and significance of management and its role in the success of the business relative to that of leadership. On examining the management and leadership literature, it appears that both concepts are concerned with the overall success of the business. Despite the continuing debate, a conclusive answer as to the respective roles and significance of management and leadership in the success of a business seems evasive. Further scrutiny of the management and leadership literature reveals a gap in comparing the content of management and leadership and their respective role(s) in the success of the business. Is either one more important than the other, and if so, to what extent; and are these concepts mutually exclusive or complementary? With the current global economic recession, information about the respective role(s) and place of management and leadership in the successful performance of the business can stand both academics and practitioners in good stead (Nienaber, 2010).

Given the divide between management and leadership, this article sought to compare the content of management and leadership, as it appears in the literature. To achieve the purpose of this article, a comprehensive literature review, utilizing a synthesis review and content analysis, was presented. This article closed with conclusions and recommendations (Nienaber, 2010).

The information presented so far suggests that nothing much has changed since the origins and first records of management and leadership. Both terms existed early in history, although they originated in different languages, and are deemed to be synonyms. Both refer to a hierarchical position in the firm that requires special qualities of the incumbent. These terms have been used interchangeably since those early days and are still being used interchangeably today (Nienaber, 2010).

There is a divide in the conceptualization of the terms *"management"* and *"leadership"* in the literature. The basis for this divide is not clear, as both management and leadership roles have a common goal and are concerned with the overall success of the business. As such, this article set out to review a range of works on classical management and leadership to determine their respective contents (Nienaber, 2010).

The findings of the literature review demonstrate that management and leadership are inextricably interwoven. All of the tasks identified in the literature reviewed fall within the boundaries of management, and the majority of these tasks overlap with leadership. Management has a few tasks that are not shared by leadership, and leadership has no distinct tasks within its boundary. These findings show that management authors, whether past or current, address most of these tasks. In the case of leadership, the contemporary authors address most of these tasks, whereas the pioneers address only some of these tasks (Nienaber, 2010).

Sanford (2011) discussed how healthcare providers use strategic planning to make their goals a reality. The focus of this article is one describing how the healthcare industry has attempted to hire and retain leadership, in their growing industry. They used human resources to help recruit and staff their facilities, which they refer to as a "people strategy" (Sanford, 2011).

Training employees correctly and finding the correct competencies for them will help maintain staffing levels. The article discussed strategic positioning and used the U.S. Army as an example. The U. S. Army has officers that move up in rank, thereby gaining more control over assets essential to the success of the military strategy. They are evaluated against their peers so the most capable candidate will move to the next strategic position. In the civilian world, every position in an organization is important to strategic positioning. For example, in the healthcare industry, every position, from volunteers to surgeons are important; they must be filled with the most capable candidates (Sanford, 2011).

Schettler (2002) covered surveys that will measure the level of importance manager's place on leadership competencies as they relate to their job. The study used 5000 managers from different industries to participate in an online study about the current state of leadership in an organization. Of those invited to participate in the survey, only 5 % responded, 80% of those that responded had some level of responsibility for leadership development, 19% of the respondents had completed responsibility for leadership development and 17% have no responsibility for leadership development. Of the respondents, 54% were male and 46% were female. These were then split evenly between upper-level, mid-level and lower-level managers (Schettler, 2002).

Leaders decided that vision is the most important part of being a leader. A visionary leader has the ability to guide others to clearly see future goals of the business and provide the necessary steps to get there. The leader must be disciplined and have a high level of creativity. A visionary leader has a strong will, is focused on his or her goal and has the tenacity to achieve his or her long term goals. They take a common goal of the organization and get the employees to follow that goal. They usually surround themselves with people who will help them reach these visionary goals and they involve their staff in attaining those goals (Schettler, 2002).

Zaleznik (1977) focused on the differences between leaders and managers. A manager is an individual who has received a title or position allows him or her the right to direct and control the behavior of others in the department. Leadership is more about interpersonal relationships and it involves inspiring, motivating, influencing and changing behaviors of others in the pursuit of a common goal. Whereas leaders embrace change; managers tend to uphold the status quo. Leaders aim for effectiveness; and managers for efficiency. Zaleznik gave several views on how managers and leaders differ. He saw leaders as inspiring visionaries concerned about substance whereas managers he viewed as planners who have concerns with process. The three audiences for the proposed study are leaders/managers, employees and the corporation/organization (Zaleznik, 1977).

Leaders would be interested because they must recognize that managerial duties are also important; managers have difficulty recognizing the interpersonal nature involved with leadership. Most researchers says that leadership can be taught and learned. Although management duties come along with the title the acts of leadership can be taught throughout an organization. Leaders and mangers, need to understand the difference between these two skills in order to know which one they need to work on to get a balanced leadership style (Zaleznik, 1992).

The second audience is the employees of the company. During questionnaire phase, employees answered questions about the leadership/management skills. The supervisors of an organization are only as good as how well they manage their employees and how well the employees perform for them. These questions, answered by the employees, will help to determine if the organization's managers are effectively leading their staff to achieve the corporation's goals. These questions will find out from employees how reasonable they think their managers are and where they see opportunities for improvement. Having the employees understand the leadership or management style being used could make their jobs easier, and they might understand their bosses' behavioral differences (Seabury, 2014).

Corporate/organizational leaders might be interested in this topic because leadership styles may need to be changed to suit specific situations. A new CEO in an established company, for example, may benefit from altering his leadership style to be more in line with the culture of his new company. Top executives themselves may need to be switched out from time to time if a company's performance establishes a pattern of decline. The best leaders do not attempt to take advantage of employees and are always ensuring that their business practices follow the most acceptable social standards and norms. With so many workers in a big business, imparting a strong sense of ethics will ensure the workers maintain the company's integrity. It is also good for shareholder and the board of directors to know so if the time comes for them to replace the CEO they can choose the best fit for the company (Richards, 2014).

According to Richards (2014), effective business leadership is critical for meeting employee, customer and business needs. Leadership skills are skills that can, fortunately, be learned. It is not true that leaders are born, not made. Business leadership skills generally center on the ability to communicate effectively, the ability to focus on the big picture, and the ability to gather and analyze information. Leadership skills in businesses are developed over time. By consistently applying leadership principles, one will begin to have dramatic effects on the organization (Richards, 2014).

Conclusion

Mainstream interest has tremendously grown over the past decade in leadership. There have been books, articles and newspapers that have been written on leadership. There has also been controversy about using mentorship programs to instill leadership qualities in those who enroll, let alone leadership courses in institutions.

Management though undoubtedly present seems to have taken a back seat. The concept of management held to date is the same as during the industrial revolution. Welch (2005) laid particular emphasis on leadership in his book "Winning," where he explored the importance of values, candor, differentiation, and voice and dignity to all.

In as much as leadership skills seem to be the priority in many business organizations, underestimating or trying to distinguish management skills is detrimental. Management skills always precede leadership skills in a formal working environment. One can possess leadership skills though not necessarily in a managerial position. That does not mean one will automatically possess management skills.

Drucker's writings have contributed to the practical foundations of the modern business corporations. Although a major portion of his work was done in the field of management he also took the time to define the role of a leader. Drucker is considered the "founder of modern management" (Denning, 2014)

CHAPTER 3: METHODOLOGY

Research refers to a search for knowledge but can also be defined as a scientific and systematic search for pertinent information on a specific topic. In fact, research is considered an art of scientific investigation (Beveridge, 1957). The design of research projects requires careful attention to the research methods and the proposed data analysis. Within this section, information is provided about the research design for the difference in leadership and management skills in an organization. There will be an overview of the research methods portion of the research proposal and then the data analysis will be addressed to show the leadership and management designs. The purpose of this methodology section is to discover answers to questions through the application of scientific procedures based on the answers given from the subjects.

Research Method and Design Appropriateness

This chapter consists of the research methodology that will be used for this study as well as how it will guide the development of theory, the collection of data and the analysis of data. On the research journey, recognition of the top five qualitative research traditions namely, biography, case study, ethnography, grounded theory and phenomenology should be addressed (Creswell, 1998). Being familiar with all of the traditions and describing all five cultures, and giving a synopsis of each that includes focus on tradition, the discipline of origin, data collection methods, data analysis method and narrative form. Creswell (1998) provides much of the general data.

A biography is the study of individual experiences as explained to the researcher and found to be true when compared with archive materials and documents (Denzin & Lincoln, 1994). Biography broadly includes biographies, autobiographies, and life and oral histories. The researcher investigates the life of one individual. Meanwhile, data is collected through many formats and in many ways, especially in the form of interviews and personal documents belonging to the person in question. Analysis of the information will take the form of stories, historical content of the individual and epiphanies, which will give a very vivid description of the life events of the person in question (Creswell, 1998).

When considering phenomenology, it is noted as the study of the shared meaning of the experience of a phenomenon for some individuals. Moustakas (1994) described it as "the understanding of meaningful, and concrete relations implicit in the original description of experience in the context of a particular situation is the primary target of phenomenological knowledge" (p. 14). The data gathered are reduced from lengthy interviews describing the shared experiences of several informants to a central meaning. In grounded theory, the researcher develops an abstract logical schema of a phenomenon. The theory then explains one of the three things, namely: an action, an interaction, or a process. Analysis occurs primarily through collecting interview data, making multiple field visits, interrelating categories of information via constant comparison, and writing a substantive or context-specific theory (Strauss & Corbin, 1990).

Furthermore, ethnography becomes an issue of concern when making such issues live. Ethnography is a study of a whole culture or social group (or an individual or individuals within a group) based primarily on observations and a prolonged period spent by the researcher in the field. The ethnographer listens and records the voices of the informants with the intent of generating a cultural portrait. When qualitative studies are conducted, case studies are done with the purpose of investigating bound systems with the goal of illustrating an issue presented within it. A proper case study always provides an in-depth analysis of the system based on the sampling of large amounts of data and data collection material. Such a system is situated within a larger setting. After getting familiar with the qualitative research traditions, grounded theory was the chosen method. The subsequent three sections describe the data collection phases for this study that consist of in-depth interviews and/or surveys.

In some cases, the use of one method outweighs the advantages of the use of another method. For example, if a person wanted to know which of two drugs was more effective, the double-blind clinical theory would be better placed than the grounded theory. However, should one want to know what it was like to be a participant in a drug study, then the ground theory would arguably provide the better option because of its qualitative nature (Strauss & Corbin, 1990)? It provides useful tools to learn about individuals' perceptions and feelings regarding a particular subject area. In this case, the objective of the research is to get the opinions of employees about management and leadership skills, and the need to distinguish them. Grounded theory methodology has the following traits similar to other qualitative methods; focus on everyday life experiences, valuing participants' perspectives, an interactive process between researcher and respondents and being primarily descriptive and relying on people's words (Glaser & Strauss, 1967). The Grounded theory originated, in the 1960s, in the fields of health. It advocated creating new theory consisting of interrelated concepts rather than focus on testing existing theories (Strauss & Corbin, 1990). A study guided by this theory aims to explain and at times even predict phenomena based on empirical data.

Population, Sampling, Data Collection Procedures and Rationale

Grounded theory uses theoretical sampling that is a form of purposive sampling, where participants are selected according to the researcher's specific criteria and based on initial findings. Data collection and analysis take place in the alternating sequence. Due to this, development and identification of variables take place as part of the data collection process. Hence, the variables are initiated by the interviewee and further developed by the researcher. All the data regarding a subject are collected until there are no new data in the area. After that, a relationship is established between the categories of data (Strauss & Corbin, 1990). Interview questions should give as little guidance as possible to allow interviewees to express what is important to them. The researcher should then extract those experiences relevant to the respondent by assigning a conceptual label known as a code. When these codes are grouped, they will eventually form the basis for the developing theory.

Coding is the first step of data analysis, as it helps to move away from detailed statements to more abstract interpretations of the interview data (Charmaz, 2006). Grounded theory methodology advocates using several coding techniques to examine interviewee's accounts. Open coding or line-by-line coding is a good starting point for identifying fundamental phenomena. Conceptual labels are attached to almost every line in the interview transcript to capture what was said. When the labels are taken from the interviewee's words, they are known as in vivo code. Strauss and Corbin (1990) suggested initial sensitizing questions that are likely to point to what data the researchers need to be led to. Some of the issues of coding include who the actors are, and what their definitions of phenomena in the study are (Strauss & Corbin, 1990).

The next phase of coding is more abstract than open coding and is known as selective coding. Focused codes are applied to several lines in a transcript and require the researcher to choose the most valid codes to represent the interviewee's voice. The aim of such coding is to add to the depth and structure of existing major categories in the information. Charmaz (2006) explained that axial coding re-assembles data that were initially broken up into separate codes through the line-to-line approach. Strauss and Corbin (1990) went on to suggest that axial coding investigates conditions of the situations described in the interview, involved actions and consequences. It is a formal and rigid framework applied to data analysis for the purpose of coding (Charmaz, 2006). Instead, they recommended the less formalized approach of reflecting on categories and sub-categories in order to establish connecting links between these to make sense of the interview data. Several rules were put forward by Glaser (1978) to develop an advanced analysis of the subject area.

Immediately after the coding of the transcripts, the researcher can identify issues of importance being raised by the respondents. These are referred to as phenomena and are assigned a conceptual label (namely a code) known as a concept according to Strauss and Corbin (1998). It should be stressed that categories have to 'earn' their way into an emerging theory (Glaser, 1978). The core category is the main one that sits at the heart of the developed theory and gives a summary, of the incident, of the research. All other broad categories should relate to the core group, which should appear frequently in the data (Strauss & Corbin, 1990). The coding process gives the analytical framework for the development of the analysis. Charmaz (2006) provided the link between coding, collection of data and developing a theory. The code provides the basis for the other two phenomena. Categories contain the analytical power of the research because of their potential to explain and predict outcomes.

The data collection for the study will be a cycle, which characterizes ground research. The survey will start by aiming to explore a broad research area on a wider scale than an interview would, while conducting it. Interviews will follow to address issues revealed by the initial survey findings. Focused coding will be utilized for the next interview phases, which will use the first codes as a basis. Axial coding will not be employed in this study because the method of specifying properties and dimensions for each category seems too prescriptive and will not help the analysis of the data. For the same reasons, theoretical coding will not be adopted. Instead, careful comparisons between respondents' statements, as well as between codes and categories will be undertaken, without being restricted to the interpretation of participants' words within a framework of properties and dimensions. The decision to use grounded theory methodology is supported by the lack of existing theory regarding leadership and management skills.

Grounded Theory methodology has evolved since its inception in the 1960s after the influential input of writers such as Glaser, Strauss and Corbin as well as Charmaz. The works of Glaser and Strauss (1967) suggested that the researcher must always begin the collection of data with a clear mind to avoid any biases. The theory will be built from observation and it needs to be 'dug up' (Charmaz, 2006). This is a point of view that assumes that every person after the researcher has a similar point of view and will come to similar conclusions. Data should be allowed to emerge by the researcher, which is the objective approach to the development of theories, which is referred to as the positivist paradigm (Charmaz, 2006).

The alternative is the constructivist approach. Charmaz (2006) also advocates for this approach where the researcher's experience comes in handy in the course of conducting the research and constructing a point of view. Knowledge is thus used by the researcher in a bid to construct the research and interpret evidence given by the research. The divergence, in the thinking, within the grounded theory arose after Glaser (1978) gave his thoughts on the approach that should be taken in the course of research approaches. Strauss and Corbin (1990) came up with a different point of view, their thoughts were that the researcher had to extrapolate the theory from the data as opposed to Glaser's view that the theory was supported by the data. It was indeed a case of which came first, the chicken or the egg.

Charmaz (2006) nonetheless found that there was common ground between the two approaches because of the external realities presented in the theories and the ability to have an objective viewpoint from both approaches. Charmaz's approach to having multiple social realities before the search for the data supported the view that the studied world needs to be presented in an interpretive way because it is a quest of the interviewee and researcher to create a reality. So, Charmaz disagreed with the initial approach that the studies conducted are neutral in any way, especially when considering the area of intangible personal privacy.

Grounded theory methodology (GMT) has limitations like any other research methodology. Some point out that GTM is very complex and time-consuming due to the tedious coding process and use of memo writing as part of the analysis. Others find that the grounded theory method is quite subjective when one is seeking to build a theory, especially depending on the researcher's sole abilities to create it. Many studies make inappropriate use of the term *grounded theory*, and the flexibility of the method can be used to provide a justification for studies lacking in methodological strength.

Sample size is dependent on considerations of the researcher related to purpose of study. The other considerations are usefulness, credibility of the selected case and available time and resources (Patton, 1980). Qualitative studies permit inquiry of selected cases with attention to detail enhancing depth. Purposeful sampling describes strategic and purposeful selection of information rich cases with the goal of making sure that the selected sample provides necessary depth but at the same time meets the goal of a preferably high degree of breadth (Patton, 1980). Because the emphasis is on quality rather than quantity, the objective is not to maximize numbers but to become "saturated" with information on the topic (Padgett, 1998, p. 52).

One survey that could be conducted is a primary data collection method which is an in-depth open-minded interview. An interview guide will be prepared to conduct the interviews. "One way to provide more structure than in the completely unstructured, informal conversational interview, while maintaining a relatively high degree of flexibility, is to use the interview guide strategy" (Patton as cited in Rubin & Babbie, 2001, p. 407). Every interview generates a subjective informative product shaped by the interviewees' experiences. The goal of qualitative interviewing is to provide understanding of what cannot be directly observed. Because qualitative interviewing assumes others perspectives to be meaningful, entering their perspectives is a major objective. Tools of observation and interviewing are often used in a complementary way (Patton, 1980).

Qualitative researchers have different classification systems for types of interviews. Patton (1980) distinguished the unstructured field interview from the more formal structured interview working with a predetermined set of open-ended questions. Patton (1980) gave details of open-ended interviews, differentiating three basic approaches: the informational conversational, standardized open-minded interview and the interview guide approach.

Table 1

Important Features of Each Interview Type

Informational conversational interview	Interview guide	Standardized open-ended interview
▪ Unstructured	▪ Semi-structured	▪ Semi-structured
▪ Questions flow from immediate context; no predetermination of questions, topic or wording	▪ The interview guide provides topics or subject areas in advance, in outline form	▪ The exact wording of questions and their sequence are predetermined
▪ Conversational flow as a major tool of fieldwork	▪ Within the framework of the guide, interviewer is free to explore	▪ Each respondent gets to answer the same questions in the same way and in the sane order, including standard probes
▪ Data gathered will be different for each person interviewed	▪ However focus on a particular predetermined subject	▪ Enhance comparability of date
	▪ Data collection more systematic	

Note. Table constructed by author using information from Patton (1980).

The format used is the interview guide approach, the wording of the questions would be pre-determined but the sequence will be determined during the conversational flow. The advantage with this style of approach is that data will be collected more systematically and all issues of interest will be covered (Patton, 1980).

Internal and External Validity

From a social constructivist point of view, the validation process involves the evaluation of the 'trustworthiness' of reported observations, interpretations, and generalizations (Mishler, 1990, p. 419). In qualitative research, the concern is with the extent to which the investigator's constructions are empirically and objectively grounded on those of the participants who are the focus of study. Internal validity refers to the validity of casual inference. There are multiple ways that the true value of the findings can be established. One can spend time with participants to check for distortions and; revise the hypotheses as more data becomes available, checking multiple sources of data such as field notes. Padgett (1998) enumerated six strategies for enhancing the rigor of the research. This research will use at least four of the strategies laying emphasis on triangulation.

External validity refers to the generalizability of the study findings. The qualitative study lays emphasis on the thick description of a relatively small number of participants in a specific setting. Samples can change as the study proceeds, but generalizations to participants are always mindful of individual lives (Padgett, 1998).

Data Analysis

The philosophical foundation of qualitative inquiry is the Interpretivist theory. Its approach is that it does not strive for universal laws because it recognizes the subjective meaning of people's experiences is what shapes reality. The analysis for the survey and interview transcripts will be based on an inductive approach. "Inductive analysis means that the patterns, themes, and categories of analysis come from the data; they emerge out of the data rather than being imposed on them prior to data collection and analysis" (Patton, 1980, p. 306).

The grounded theory method will be employed in this study. "A grounded theory is one that is inductively derived from the study of the phenomenon it represents. That is, it is discovered, developed, and provisionally verified through systematic data collection and analysis of data pertaining to that phenomenon" (Strauss & Corbin, 1990, p. 23). Data will be analyzed using the constant comparative method (Strauss & Corbin, 1990) whereby line, sentence, and paragraph segments of the transcribed interviews and field notes will be reviewed to decide what codes fit the concepts suggested by the data.

Available qualitative data analysis (QDA) programs included ATLAS.ti, The Ethnograph, HyperQual, HyperRESEARCH, NUD*IST, and NVivo. The interest for this research is in the ATLAS.ti QDA software, and will be used in the dissertation research for data organization and management.

Summary

The research is meant to determine the need to distinguish leadership and managements skills by organizations. A qualitative mode of research is what is deemed appropriate in trying to answer the research questions. The specific data collection methods deemed appropriate for this kind of study were interviews and surveys. The interviews will have a set of pre-determined questions asked to all the interviewees in the same manner. Data collected by conducting structured interviews are perceived to be associated with a high level of validity, due to the fact that each member of the sample group is asked the same questions, therefore, there are fewer chances for the interviewees to be biased.

CHAPTER 4: RESULTS, ANALYSIS, AND FINDINGS

Due to the increasing desire for effectiveness and competitive coverage in firms, it is very simple to concentrate on the immediate factor for the increase and pay less focus to the other systemic factors that may not have an apparent influence on the prosperity of businesses. Thus, one of those important areas is the leadership and management development. Leadership needs an exceptional vision for accomplishment as well as the tools that are essential for the process of communication and execution of those ideas. There is need for administrators to consider the strategies that will ensure that effective skills and competencies are incorporated in the leadership within the organization. Thus, leaders must have a series of vividly defined principles and the daring skills to transform the visions into realities. When they include employees in their undertakings then the set objectives of the organization will be achieved synergistically. For this reason, many people trust that very favorable development of leadership skills occur when the leader works towards the growth of social construct as well as the success of the company.

Situation Assessment

This study was conducted to ascertain the effects of the nature of leadership skills in an organization and the general performance of employees and leaders. The leadership and management skills in an enterprise act as the fundamental basis that make and drive respective passions that several individuals cherish. There exists circumstances when leaders have altered their objectives and seems to be solely concerned with the financial returns. With experienced leadership, everybody in the company is sure that somebody they believe in is working in the desired direction. Within this kind of structures in place, some of the most crucial aspects for the success of leaders is the installation of belief among from other teammates as well as employees (William, 2011). Real leadership must involve steering the group places that such members would not attempt to reach on their own. Attaining this kind of dedication and loyalty is tough without real allegiance, motivated by the aspects of true leadership skills. Many companies instinctively recognize that they can perform better when they develop such skills and inculcate them in their organization as the foundation of success. On the other hand, traditional pieces of literature on organization and leadership theory has been dominated nearly entirely by the perception that leadership is something held by just one person; the notion of the unified command. However, this has been exclusively challenged by new theoretical framework of the post-heroic leadership that suggests that the act of leadership is a corporate affair rather than being held by a single person (William, 2011).

Moreover, the concerns of the organization revolves around the need of adequate leadership within the framework of operation. There is the need to advocate for effective leadership and management to ascertain the existence of necessary competencies and skills that will guarantee the attainment of the set objectives and strategies (Ganesan, 2010). The annual costs that companies will incur from lack of current leadership will continue to grow if the organizations will not identify the challenges and deficiencies in the direction and management domains. The element of effective leadership is supposed to incorporate a personal desire to improve the employees and achieve the objectives with limited resources by utilizing the changing worldviews and behaviors within the corporate scope. Leadership and management growth and development are persuasive in nature and, therefore, more time should be spent in evaluating performance and effectiveness at personal and organizational levels. The degree to which the purposes of an organization are attained depends on the nature, composition, and implementation of the leadership skills. The leaders should focus on the overall participation of each member and full commitment to the plans and strategies of the enterprise (Fred Garcia, 2006). However, a significant challenge emanates from the lack of the necessary skills that are in line with the culture of the organization.

Management expertise and corporate strategy play a key role in the organization and this study; the leaders had to provide a description of accounts when they supported their managers in achieving the objectives of the organization's goals in the capacities they served. There are reasons why organizations do not consider the support offered by leaders to managers a vital tool for effectiveness. The competencies that are needed in an organization to help the directors of high-performance undertakings are involved and spill over to other duties within the organization causing the overlapping of mandates. The process of helping managers is a required multi-dimensional skill that will guarantee the operation of solving problems. Moreover, the exposition considered the support of leaders to the regulatory activities as vital because organizations are in need of developed full-range leadership experiences that will incorporate mentorship activities, rotational assignments, feedback systems, and relationship development in a working environment. However, it is not easy to achieve such a scenario in corporate sector because tasks and challenges experienced in the jobs and interaction with employees while undertaking the objective activities are associated with learning that is not equal regarding development and growth of skills.

The argument of whether the managerial and leadership skills should be combined was examined in the study. The investigation of the topic depicted the notion of the overlapping of expertise attached to direction and management such as those depicted in nursing professional (Sullivan, 2012). However, the reason for the amalgamation will depend on the emerging issues in the process of change in the organization. The problem lies in the belief that when leaders and managers improve the knowledge and skills of their employees that relate to the objectives of the organization, then they are guaranteed of an increase in output and effectiveness. The interpersonal relationships of individuals play a significant role in the extent to which performance can be measured. The skills of a manager is exclusively relevant and contribute to the total percentage of success as the leadership competencies at a personal level. The study examined the perception of the employees on the direction methodologies of their supervisors and linked responses to the commitment of the directors in assisting their managers to achieve the organization's objective as defined in the strategic plans. Therefore, it is necessary for a clear understanding whether the leadership competencies and managerial skills should be merged in any organization.

Key Factors

Training of the groups in an organization was a factor that was examined in the study. The leaders and managers are mandated to offer to train to ensure that they know how to reach their goals. The research examined how leaders and managers exercised their duty by building competencies to their members and followers. The effective participation in an organization does not call for directing the main actors, but it requires skills that will enable them to embrace the point of view of their leaders and managers. Organizations operate on plans and strategies that are inclined towards establishing and sustaining a corporate culture that should be followed by the members attached to the enterprise. The team in the organization is to be trained to embrace change and implement strategies (Relevant development: Effective leadership training, 2012). The managers who exercise sound management training activities enjoy the accrued advantages of successful operations (Hersey & Blanchard, 1996). The process of training assists the team being lead to master the process of problem analysis and decision-making.

The study also considered the availability of managers and leaders because it is one of the essential elements of success. The participants were asked whether their leaders or managers were available for consultations or inquiries. When leaders and managers are available in the organization the level of errors when undertaking duties is reduced. The process of managing the availability calls for a succinct analysis according to the necessity of the services that needs consultations. Therefore, the leaders and managers should avoid the circumstances where the workers and followers manipulate them. The level of leadership or management position determines the nature of availability hence should not be confused with supervision (Fiedler, 1996; Needed: Transformational leaders, 2002). The process of delegation of duties assists in time management. However, leadership and management do not offer availability as an option because it is necessary to ensure that the leaders and manager are conversant within their scope of operation.

Moreover, the study considered the concept of approachability of leaders and managers because it helps in determining whether their undertakings will lead to effectiveness. Being approachable is associated with the comfort and courage of employees. The notions of leadership and management do not involve the element of isolation. When a leader is friendly, it does not mean that they are accepted and liked by the members of their group, but rather they can be informed the occurrences of the organization and can listen to people (Cooper, 2014). Being approachable entails building a warm environment while on duty to allow the subjects to connect whenever there is the need. Friendly leaders and managers do not overreact to bad news and will always appreciate being informed of the pursuits going on in the business. When one maintains consistent actions and cuts down on sarcasm, they can make approachable managers. The leaders thus must have a series of vividly defined principles and the daring skills to transform the visions to become realities.

The notion of feedback was also another factor considered in the study. The respondents were asked the frequency with which they receive reports from their managers and leaders on their performance, progress, and recommended changes. The aspect of feedback influences the effectiveness of leadership and management (DeRue & Wellman, 2009). The organizations should have a feedback system that incorporates the needs of diversity. Feedback from leaders and managers should involve three main elements: the sources of feedback, the content, and the recipient. Feedback is useful if it is time bound. The employees and team members are motivated when constant communication culture is created in the organization ensuring that they are informed of their performance, progress, and the changes they need to implement to improve them [productivity and competence. It should be the desire of every manager or leader to raise their effectiveness by incorporating quality feedback to ensure that they inspire progress and save on time (DeRue & Wellman, 2009).

Events

The study assessed the leadership ability of managers. The respondents gave their perceptions relating to the leaders and managers they are working under their authority.

The responses they gave were used to set the baseline for conclusions and the extent to which the objective of the study was met. Employees determined the answers that guided the study topic. Employees were asked to rate the leadership ability of their managers using an ordinal like the Likert scoring system, where a score of strongly agree, agree, neutral, disagree and strongly disagree indicates leadership characteristics displayed by the manager. The range of score assisted the participants to rate their leaders based on their interaction and experience. The employees associate with their bosses and are in a position to give a firsthand account on their abilities to lead the organization plans towards economic achievements. To establish a foundation for the study, survey questions were developed and were proved or disproved based on the accounts throughout the process of inquiry. The application of the Likert scale determined the rate of leadership skills and introduced substantial qualitative data component to the study while the elements stem from participant response, specifically the quality of a manager's leadership ability within the work environment. The study made meaningful achievement by utilizing the range of diversity inclusion that is available when the Likert scale is used.

The process of implementing the inferential statistics within the study involved two phases. The statistics were divided into two groups and the process of filtering and sorting the data depended on the response made by the participants. The researcher, therefore, differentiated between two groups. The first group believed that the managers and leaders demonstrated leadership skills in the work environment. The first category deemed the activities of their leaders as the best undertakings towards the achievement of the set goals and objectives. The group believed that the leaders did their best to ensure that a sustainable corporate environment for mutual professional integration was created.

The group involved all the indicator of a rating above 'neutral'. The second group did not believe that the manager represented a leader and was indicated by a score below 'neutral.' It is not possible to examine the entire population individually and, therefore, a sample size that represented the population characteristics was used for this study. The randomly sampled group of respondents involved a size of 100 employees, and 60 executives participated in the study. A confidence interval of 95% was used as a tool to measure statistical data based on the responses collected from the sample sizes that included employees and executives.

The responses from the employees were used as the baseline to determine whether businesses need to focus on differentiating leadership from management to achieve effective overall corporate strategies. The employees responded to questions that pertained to the efficiency of their managers and leaders. The workers rated the effectiveness of the training they received from their supervisor. The training they were to consider included those meant to orient, prepare, and equip with necessary skills and competencies towards the strategy of the organization. The respondents also rated the availability of their leaders and managers to the needs of the employees and how approachable did, they perceive their supervisors. Moreover, the participants rated their level of improvement regarding performance after getting feedback from their supervisor about the work they were doing. Besides, the employees gave an account of how often they received feedback about their work from their managers and leaders.

On the other hand, the executives who participated in the study responded to several questions. The objective of interviewing the leaders was to get their perception of the notion of leadership and management. The information gathered from the leaders was used to determine the existence of a correlation between the management skills and leadership competencies. The executives gave an account of their influence on employees to follow the strategic vision for the organization. The leaders explained whether they had changed positivity among their followers and subjects. The managers were also asked on the occasions when they demonstrated the most important values and ethics as a leader to influence and inspire the employees, and they accompanied the scenarios with practical examples within the various organizational setups. The executives were also asked to cite some situations in which a leader may fail and expound on situations if any when they had failed as a leader. Moreover, the executives were asked to state the roles that leadership played as a manager and how they had exercised the same with their managers. Besides, the leaders have been invited to give an account of the methodologies they had used to gain commitment from their team.

Findings

The study found that the answers from the questions asked during the research varied with the objective of the question designed. The diversity of the replies assisted in depicting the reality of the concept of leadership and management in the organization. Women and men who participated in the investigation gave varied answers on the same factor. The following tables provide a summary of the responses to each factor involving the perception of employees on their leaders in the organization according to the gender.

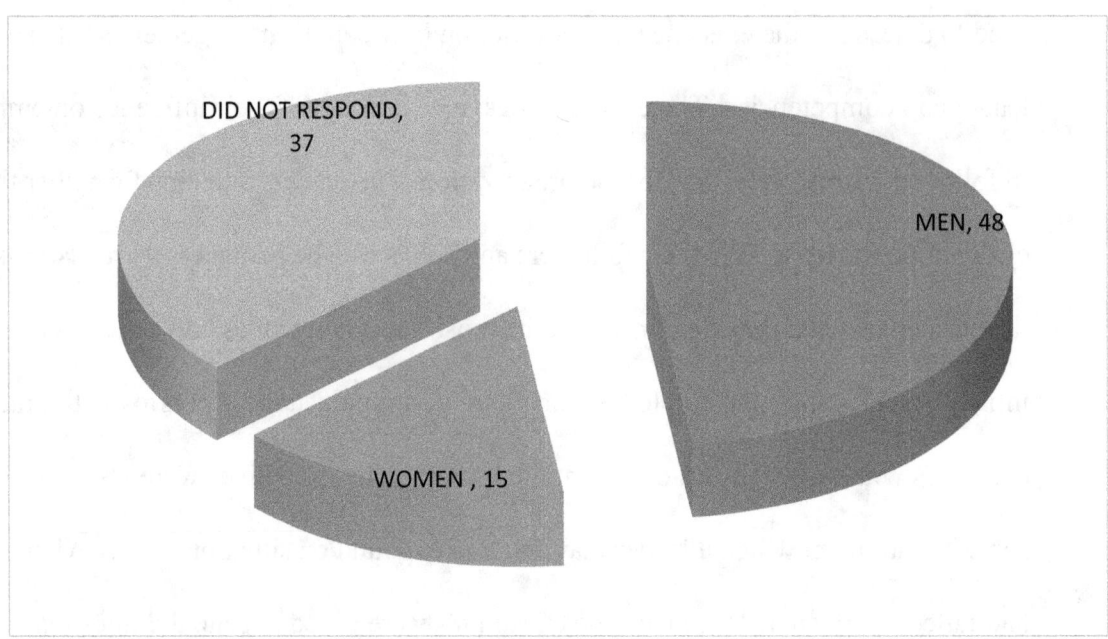

Figure 1. Employee response percentages.

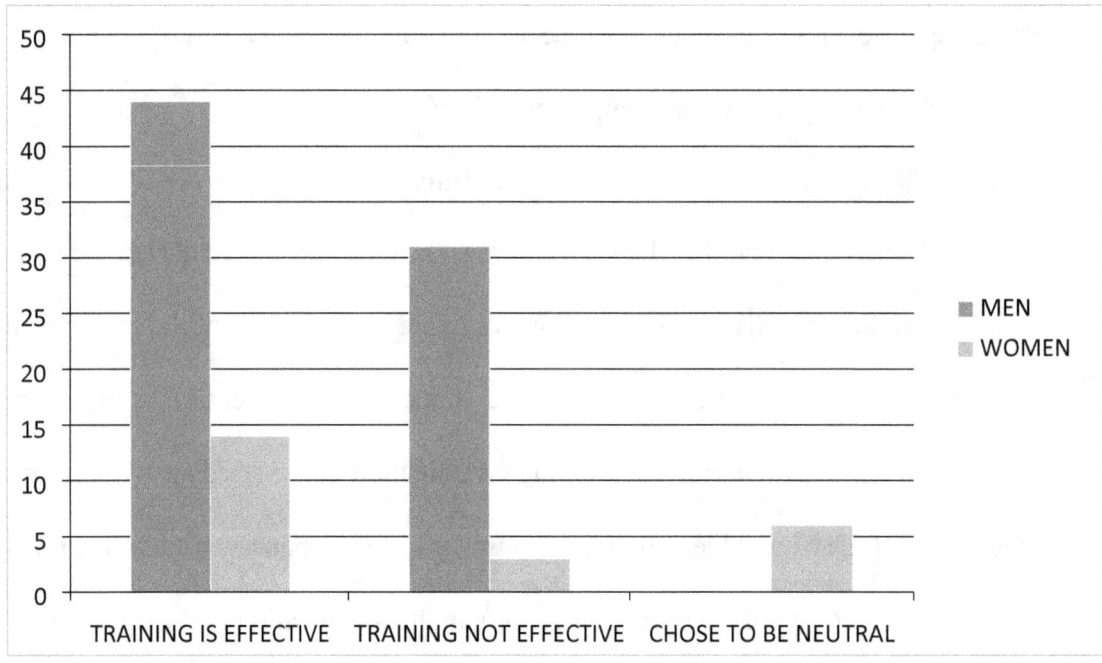

Figure 2. Employee percentages response on the training from supervisors.

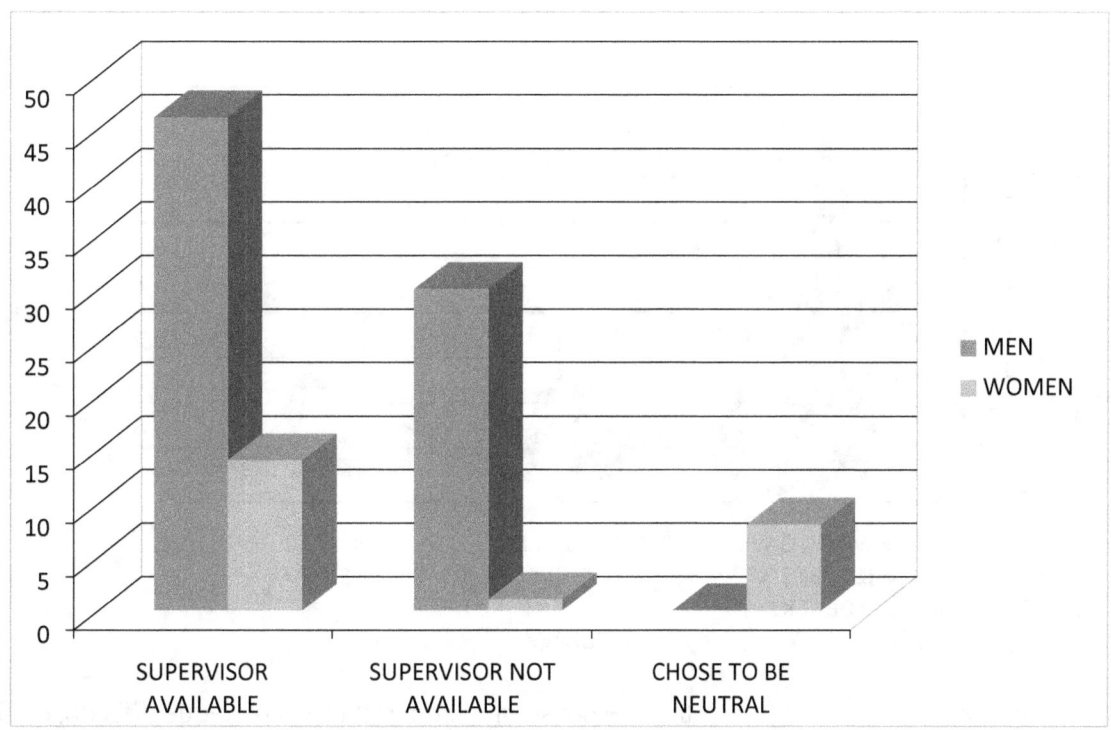

Figure 3. Employee percentage response on the availability of supervisors.

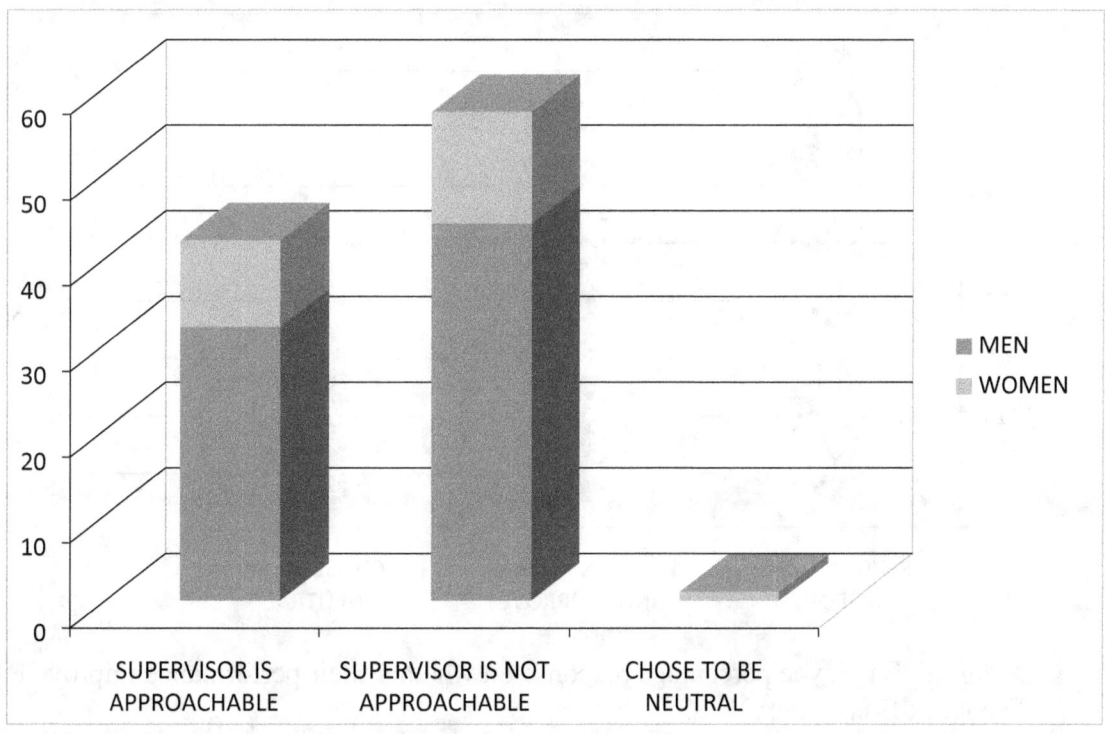

Figure 4. Employee percentage response on the approachability of supervisors.

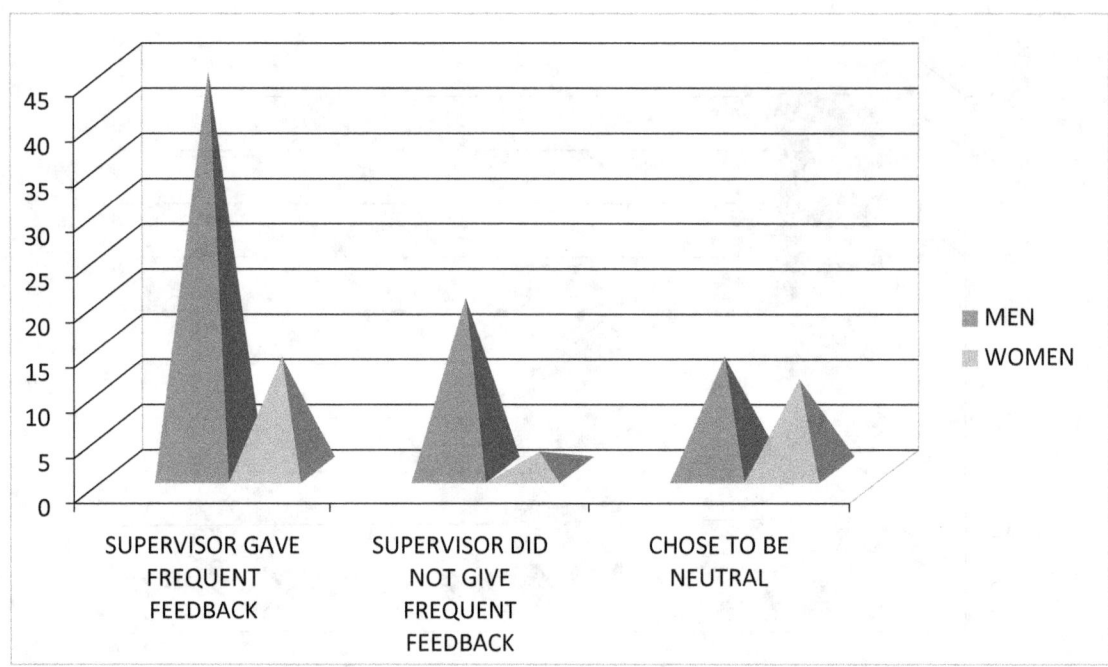

Figure 5. Employee percentage response on whether there was frequent feedback from supervisors.

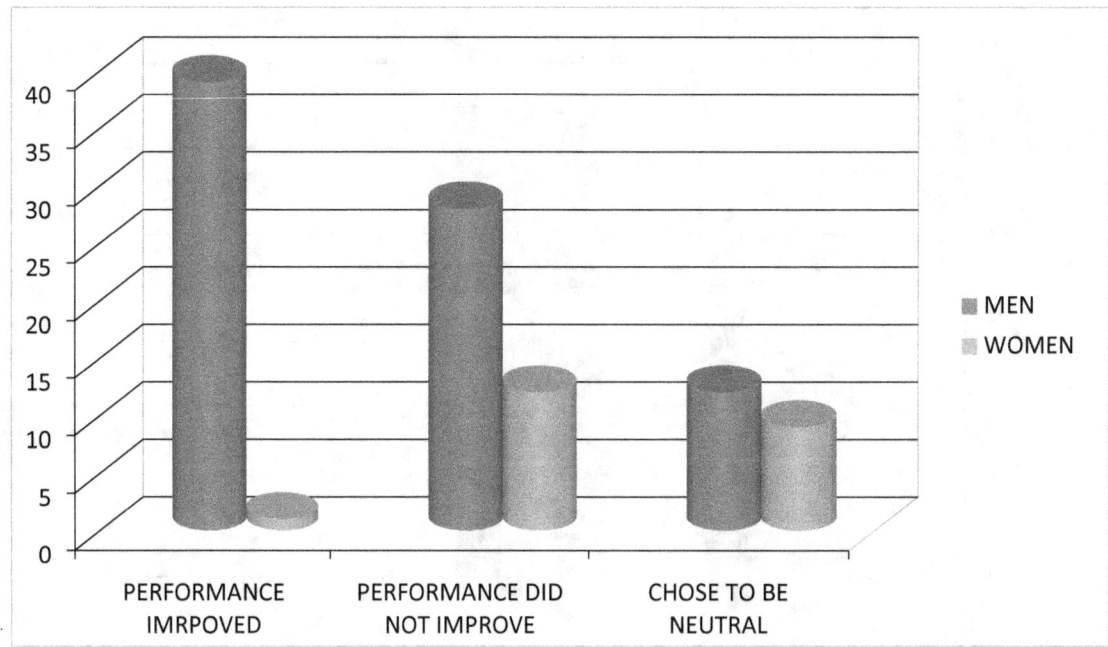

Figure 6. Employee percentage response on whether their performance improved After Feedback from supervisors.

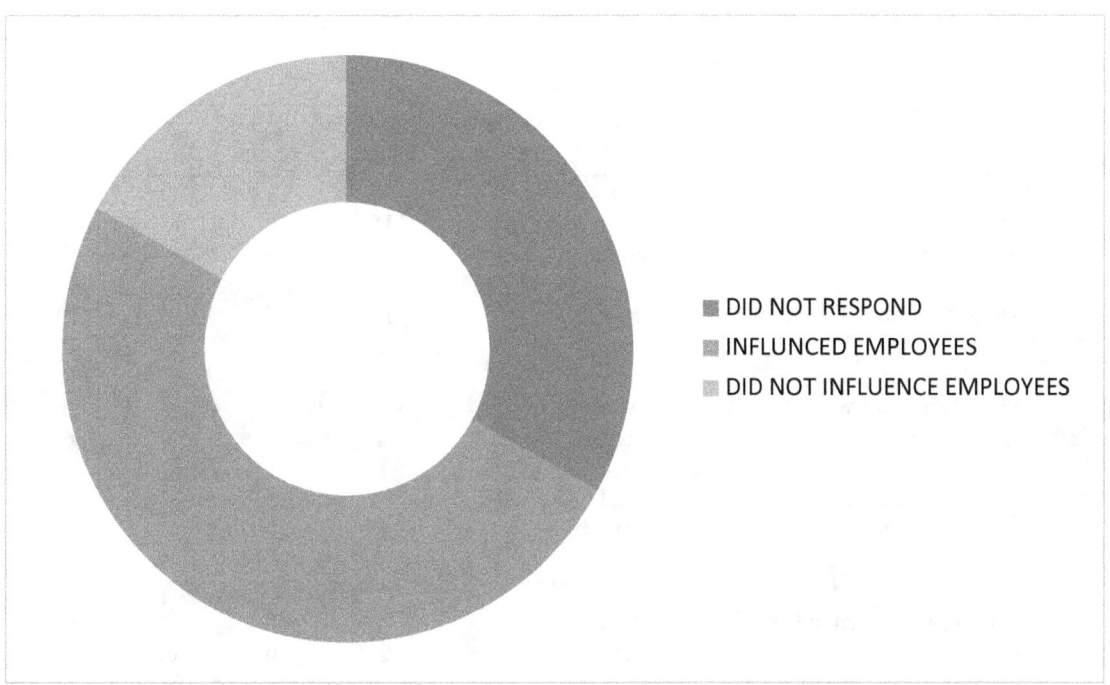

Figure 7. Executive percentage response on whether they have been influencing their employees.

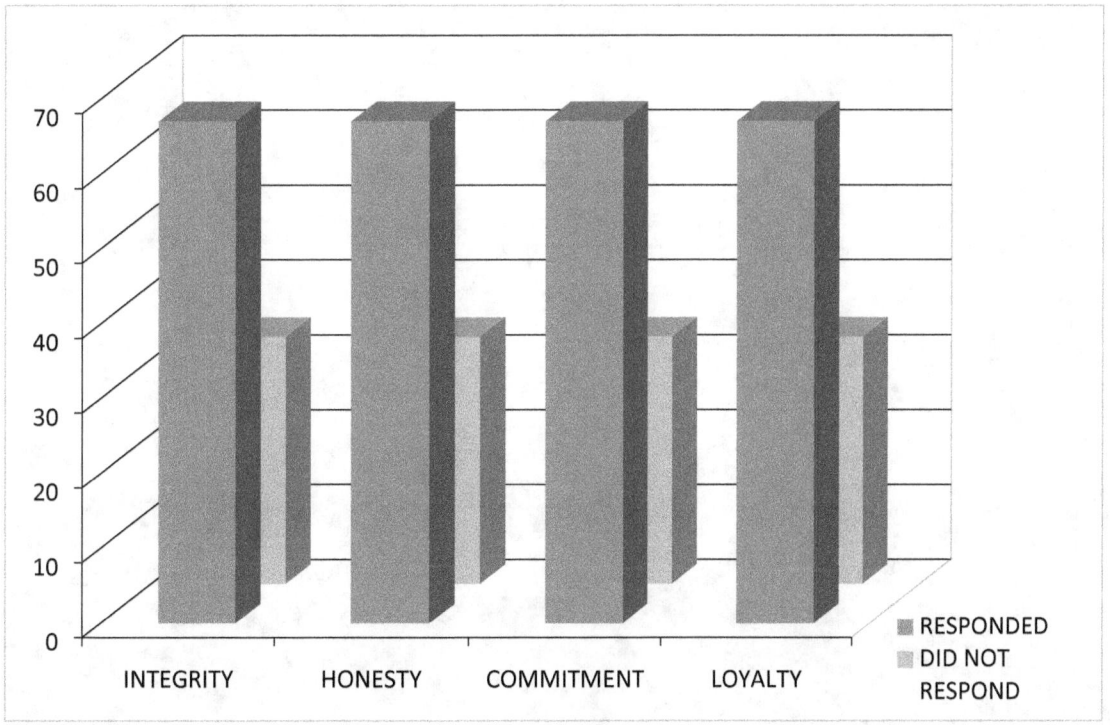

Figure 8. Executive percentage response on the qualities they value.

Table 2

Summary of Employees Responses

Factor	Gender[a]	Strongly disagree	Disagree	Neutral	Agree	Strongly agree
The training from supervisors was effective	Men	5	15	0	12	16
	Women	0	2	4	0	9
The supervisors were available	Men	9	10	0	10	19
	Women	0	1	5	0	9
The supervisors were approachable	Men	18	10	0	12	8
	Women	0	8	1	0	6
Their performance improved after getting feedback from supervisors	Men	0	18	5	12	13
	Women	0	5	8	1	1
Supervisors gave feedback frequently	Men	0	12	8	12	16
	Women	6	2	6	0	1

[a] Total of 63/100 responded.

Description of What Was Found

The above section entailed the detailed account of the findings of the study. The qualitative exposition was aimed at identifying the effect of leadership skills and management competencies in an organization as well as the perception of both the employees and their leaders on the activities inclined on managerial leadership. The study has shown that the elements and factors of leadership are vital in the process of registering effectiveness in organizations. The results revealed that an organization could only achieve the intended objectives if they are concerned about the way leadership activities and methodologies are implemented. Both male and female respondent agreed that the manner in which a leader carries out the daily routine in a working environment determined the extent of their commitment and expertise while working. The study considered five factors that touched on the employee-leader relationship. The elements of training, availability, and approachability of supervisors showed the need for more changes in the leadership strategies employed in the organization. The inclusion of feedback and the impact created when employees receive reports on their performance assisted in depicting the growth and development of professionalism ignited by leaders and managers (Krasman, 2009).

The respondents believed that they received the required training from their supervisors in line with the required objectives and activities of the organization. The employees ascertained the fact that the knowledge regarding the analytic processes in the body was essential for them to meet the set targets in the respective work plans. The leaders are entitled to powers that enable them to explain the strategic objectives of the organization to the employees to ensure that they are familiar with the undertakings in the business (Sinclair & Sinclair, 2004). Whenever the employees are trained on the strategy requirements of the organization as well as the internal processes, then they will be part

of the entire course by owning the objectives scaled down to departmental levels and

eventually to individual capacity (Mann, 2006). Employees need feedback on their

performance each time they are appraised. The study revealed that a mechanisms set by

leaders for effective feedback communication assist employees in improving their

performance by correlating their activities to the recommendations made by their

supervisors. Besides, it was noted that workers are motivated to deliver more quality and

quantity whenever leaders recognize their efforts.

Moreover, the study revealed that the employees expect the leaders to be mentors

and role models. The executives who responded to the research question also

acknowledged their duty in influencing their followers towards attaining high goals. The

study ascertained the fact that the availability of leaders is essential to ensuring the

workers remain within the scope of operation while in a working environment. The

respondents affirmed that their leaders were available for whenever needed. Leaders and

managers who are always available for consultation and information relating to feedback

on the duties to be undertaken allow more progress to accompany the activities of the

organization on a daily basis. The study showed how the availability of a leader assists in

setting up a culture of constant commitment to duty. Besides, the study linked the

approachability of the supervisors to the mutual corporate coexistence in the

organization. It is the accountability of the leader to build a sense of friendship and

openness in the team within the organization (Watson & Reissner, 2010). The objective

of being approachable is to create an environment that will ensure that the employees feel

comfortable and acceptable while working within the team. The study showed a correlation between the approachability of a supervisor with the progress of a particular group in an organization.

The responses from the executive demonstrated how the leaders and manager play a vital role in ensuring that the organization operates in a sustainable culture. The study showed the need for organizations to allow the designing of a leadership scheme based on personality and characteristics. The personal attributes are linked to leadership effectiveness. Each employee in the institution recognized that the personal characteristics of leaders such as honesty and integrity influenced their leadership effectiveness. The team leaders are expected to build their individual awareness and consciousness of colleagues. Each crew chief is tasked to learning adjustments of their style to house the followers. The executives gave accounts on occasions when they were to choose between being honest and exercising greed. All leaders affirmed that they were expected to watch the extent to which they are outgoing, social, talkative and the way they express emotions. For example, leaders confirmed that they are scheduled to show trust, understanding, compassion, cooperation, and affection. The concept explains why for one to become a leader, he/she is tested to determine whether he/she is considerate, goal-oriented, organized, and attentive to specifics. The leaders are expected to strive and stabilize their emotions and moods. Besides, leaders are called to share their imaginative and insightful power and their curiosity (Ivonne, 2010). The study showed that the leaders play a critical role in inspiring the employees and being there for help when needed to ensure that the process of the attaining objectives is in line with the defined inputs, activities, and expected outputs.

Comparison

Leadership is the capacity to impact followers and supporters on attaining a common goal and objective through shared determinations (Schroeder & Lombardo, 2013). Without the members who constitute the group to be lead, a leader will not be considered as a valid entity. A leader is one capable of creating an impact on a group of people to realize goals and purpose. The driving force of the head and the subjects is the intended objective that will guide the scope of operation as well as the activities to be carried put. Those under the influence of a leader are called followers (Schroeder & Lombardo, 2013). Scholars have explained many leadership theories over years. The methods are analyzed basing on the studies carried out. Depending on the circumstance, methods of implementation, and parties involved principles of management are defined.

When talking about leadership parties should understand the meaning of a common goal. Whenever the two sides are focused towards the same purpose, then the process of attaining the set objectives will be easy. Standard meaning refers to an anticipated future or ends circumstances of the organization (Schroeder & Lombardo, 2013). A common aim aids leaders and followers to familiarize themselves in a similar direction. However, it is not acceptable to associate shared purpose to a common objective. Shared tenacities speak more to how a leader and followers are destined to common goals. An effective leader is one who does the necessary task to grasp a common goal or achieve surprising results. Effective leadership, if all parameters are objectively structured, is the core of success and effectiveness in an organization. Some factors affect the engagements of followers and the leader. The principles guiding the operation of the group are different from the beliefs of the leader (Schroeder & Lombardo, 2013).

Leadership is bound to some repetitive guidelines and norms. Excellence is derived from the understanding of the working environment. The principles setting the baseline for motivation and commitment are defined in the guides and routine. Effective leaders should understand the principles governing leadership. Leadership involves taking the responsibility for making decisions, bringing change, and empowering people to discover and use their potential. Leadership entails setting examples. Excellence in orientation is prodigious to stimulate development. Leaders should not only inform members what to do but also, show by example. During complicated situations, leaders should step out with confidence and determination. Leaders should make impacts apart from the setting of goals (Mendez-Morse, 2004). They should go beyond impressive achievements. Leadership should make a positive change.

Besides, leadership calls for clear vision. When leaders and followers are working towards achieving a sustainable culture or completing a particular mission, then they will escape the effect of complexity and stagnation. Leaders should devote their efforts and time to the apprehension of the vision. Vision is defined as inspiring organizations to take action and forge forward because it acts as the roadmap for the activities intended to be accomplished (Wilson, 1997). Leaders should inspire every member of the team with that vision. Each member of the group has a part to play in the process of scoring the intended grade. The objectives of the organization are based on the individual effort cumulatively perceived as the full achievement of the group.

Depending on circumstances, leaders should embrace flexibility in tasks and communication. Flexibility is a useful trait that helps one's decisions to be based on the value system (1, 2, & Du 3, 2014). Leading involves communication, influence, and engagements and therefore, leaders should prioritize the people. The active leader admits mistakes and gives room for learning (Schroeder & Lombardo, 2013). Leadership will be effective if teamwork and unity are upheld. Embracing teams and devoting one's energy guarantee achievements. Satisfaction should be short-term because ambitions are useless without improvements.

Management entails the identification of the organization's missions, visions, aims, objectives, procedures, and rules. Managers look into the best proportion to incorporate the resources available to ensure the intentions of the organization is realized. Management activities manipulate the human capital to build success and sustainability of an enterprise. The active management environment implies that the human motivation, successful progress, and system outcomes are conspicuous (Schroeder & Lombardo, 2013). It should be noted that control could occur in a legal or illegal framework; however, it does not manipulate mechanism rather it exercises and implement the factors of the mechanism.

Since management involves the improvement of relationship and lives, it should not be considered as an institutions affair. Management is a multifaceted phenomenon that can be widely applied to achieve the desired goals. The components of management are communication, the humans, and the endeavors of the organization. Therefore, the managers should develop skills that will enable a healthy interaction with the management team to ensure that they work towards the purpose of the organization. The undertakings of the group are outlined in the plans, economic measurements, motivational strategies, and the goals. Management processes incorporate the measuring of quantity and quality, adjustments of plans, and meeting the goals. The functions of management include aspects such as forecasting, planning, organizing, commanding, coordinating, and controlling.

Enlightenment Offered by Key Players

Effective leadership and management are cultivated upon grasping a wide assortment of skill. The skills range from implementation, policies making and establishing procedures. The expertise should be used to motivate staff to achieve essential criterions. Besides the tangible advantages, working as team points to great contentment. The pleasure derived will correlate with promising structural results. An active and efficient leader or manager will always be willing to work with others in groups and agreements to make mediation that is more momentous. The forerunners believe that no party can be able to make it alone unless they work as a team. The frontrunner can picture a range of opportunities ahead of the current phase of development (Schroeder & Lombardo, 2013).

Furthermore, effective leaders and managers should have a great sagacity of timing; they are patient and willing to wait until the time is right to make a significant interpolation to strike and achieve decisively. He/she is always alert and prepared to seize a prospect. The parties invest in time developing people, their capability and for the future of the organization. Besides, he/she will manage the current needs of the institution. The best leaders and managers believe in pragmatism leading all the departmental heads to strategize developments that lead to tactics. The tactics developed and outlined, will eventually incorporate the vision, mission, and objectives for the success of the organization. The strategies are based on a rational appraisal of the situation utilizing available resources and the opportunities that exist to maximize outputs and realize goals (Schroeder & Lombardo, 2013).

The concept of effective decision-making is a critical tool for organizations to step outside normal patterns of thinking, make innovative solutions, and generate great ideas. Leaders should consider brainstorming as a method of generating ideas (Dunsford, 2003). People outside the organization might influence or be affected by decisions made in an organization. Leaders should learn how to make practical decisions. When leaders are making decisions, they need to have enough information to avoid biases. The leaders should take some time to gather the necessary data to inform their decision but avoid conflicting information. When avoiding analysis parallelism, the parties involved should decide the information that is required and set timescale for decision-making. It is worth to know the views of other people. Decisions need the prospect of change, and people find it difficult (Schroeder & Lombardo, 2013). Therefore, leaders and managers should have in mind that the complexity of finding solution increases with increase in the number of people involved. Moreover, when making a decision, they should understand the problem, the causes, and expected impacts if interventions are not employed. Understanding the problem ensures a higher probability of finding the solutions. A problem solved without considering where it emanated from will still have a possibility of re-occurrence. Creating a list of possible solutions will enable the leader to have the most appropriate and efficient solution (Bryant, 2003). Once a leader or a manager is contended with the selection of realistic alternatives; an evaluation of the feasibility, risks, and implications is done. Next is to make the decision by choosing the best option. When implementing the decision, it is important to monitor the effectiveness of the solution continuously. Problem-solving is an essential component of leadership and management skills.

Effective leadership and management skills should provide avenues for the association of complementary stimulation and elevation that are geared towards transforming followers into leaders. Leadership arises when individuals in a team engage in transforming one another through integrative mechanisms. As managers, leaders, and follower cooperate and interrelate during their duties, they build each member to high levels of enthusiasm and standards by improving their competence. An effective leadership approach is enhanced through proposed mechanisms that have the potential to shape, alter, and elevate the motives, ideals, and goals. Through the set policies, followers can achieve momentous transformation and progress if leaders engage in a mutual coexistence. The system set forth in an organization is able to acknowledge the existence of an extraordinary strength entangled in modifying leadership principle and support employees through mentorship and motivational undertakings. For example, managers can convert leaders into people who uphold right, desire to achieve, and values because it is advised that the leaders should share freely information with members. The self-interest of deputies is deemed paramount and transformed into real dreams. Leaders should undertake activities that can increase followers' confidence. Preeminent followers' desires, expectations, and heightening the value of the leadership create outcomes for the member. Moreover, leaders should encourage behavioral change and motivate others to higher levels of individual accomplishment.

Summary

Concerns of the organization revolve around the need of adequate leadership within the framework of operation. There is the need to advocate for effective leadership and management to ascertain the existence of necessary competencies and skills that will guarantee the attainment of the set objectives and strategies. The study assessed the leadership ability of managers. The respondents gave their perceptions relating to the leaders and managers they are working under their authority. The responses they gave were used to set the baseline for conclusions and the extent to which the objective of the study was met. Employees determined the answers that guided the study topic. Employees were asked to rate the leadership ability of their managers using an ordinal like the Likert scoring system, where a score of strongly agree, agree, neutral, disagree and strongly disagree indicates leadership characteristics displayed by the manager. The randomly sampled group of respondents involved a size of 100 employees, and 60 executives participated in the study. A confidence interval of 95% was used as a tool to measure statistical data based on the responses collected from the sample sizes that included employees and executives. The study considered five factors that touched on the employee-leader relationship. The elements of training, availability, and approachability of supervisors showed the need for more changes in the leadership strategies employed in the organization. The inclusion of feedback and the impact created when employees receive reports on their performance assisted in depicting the growth and development of professionalism ignited by leaders and managers.

CHAPTER 5: CONCLUSION

Leadership development is an area that most companies and organizations must take keen focus on to enable them achieves huge milestones in their business plans. As a result, the questions of the study contributed to the knowledge of improving any leadership deficits that might be identified in the administrative capacity. The research questions were significant in helping evaluate the usefulness of the situational approach and skills regarding the notion of shared leadership that has been very underdeveloped in many kinds of literature and in organization. The research questions gave the findings that unfolded the aspects of leadership skills that many other companies will consider essential in their fields and may adopt to improve their weak areas for such companies to realize their business objectives. There is need for administrators to consider the strategies that will ensure that effective skills and competencies are incorporated in the leadership within the organization. The leaders thus must have a series of vividly defined principles and the daring skills to transform the visions to become realities. When they include the employees in their undertakings then the set objectives of the organization will be achieved synergistically.

Conclusions

The study assessed the leadership ability of managers. The respondents gave their perceptions relating to the leaders and managers, whose authority they are working under. The responses they gave were used to set the baseline for conclusions and the extent to which the objective of the study was met. Employees determined the answers that guided the study topic. Employees were asked to rate the leadership ability of their managers using an ordinal like the Likert scoring system, where a score of strongly agree, agree, neutral, disagree and strongly disagree indicates leadership characteristics displayed by the manager. The responses from the employees were used as the baseline to determine whether businesses need to focus on differentiating leadership from management to achieve effective overall corporate strategies.

The employees responded to questions that pertained to the efficiency of their managers and leaders. On the other hand, the executives who participated in the study responded to several questions. The objective of interviewing the leaders was to get their perception of the notion of leadership and management. The information gathered from the leaders was used to determine the existence of a correlation between the management skills and leadership competencies. The executives gave an account of their influence on employees to follow the strategic vision for the organization.

The study focused on four factors of employee-supervisor engagements: training, availability, approachability, and feedback Training of the groups in an organization was a factor that was examined in the study. The leaders and managers are mandated to offer to train to ensure that they know how to reach their goals. The research examined how leaders and managers exercised their duty by building competencies to their members and followers. The study also considered the availability of executives and leaders because it is one of the essential elements of success.

The participants were asked whether their leaders or managers were available for consultations or inquiries. When leaders and managers are available in the organization the level of errors when undertaking duties is reduced. Moreover, the study considered the concept of approachability of leaders and managers because it helps in determining whether their undertakings will lead to effectiveness. Being approachable is associated with the comfort and courage of employees. The notions of leadership and management do not involve the element of isolation. The concept of feedback was also another factor considered in the study. The respondents were asked the frequency with which they receive reports from their managers and leaders on their performance, progress, and recommended changes. The aspect of feedback influences the effectiveness of leadership and management (DeRue & Wellman, 2009).

The study found that the skills of leaders are essential for effective performance in an organization. Leadership is the capacity to impact followers and supporters on attaining a common goal and objective through shared determinations (DeRue & Wellman, 2009). The research affirmed that the leader should drive the members towards achieving the set goals and objectives as outlined in the vision of the enterprise. Without the members who constitute the group to be lead, a leader will not be considered as a valid entity. A leader is one capable of creating an impact on a group of people to realize goals and purpose. Depending on circumstances, leaders should embrace flexibility in tasks and communication. Flexibility is a useful trait that helps one's decisions to be based on the value system. Leading involves communication, influence, and engagements and therefore, leaders should prioritize the people. Moreover, recognizes that mistakes are proof that something is being done. Active leader admits mistakes and gives room for learning. The leaders also play an essential role in supporting the managers to undertake their duties. The roles played by the leaders and managers are distinct in nature and the skills requires could be similar. However, the equal mix of each competency varies.

Furthermore, the study concluded that leadership involves planning, scheduling, controlling, and working together with the followers on various duties. Without effective leaders who can support the employees and the managers, neither assistance nor organizational goals would be implemented. Leadership pursues to maintain solidity because the styles used focuses on maintenance of steady and quality routine from members to attain organizational goals and objectives (Bryant, 2003). Real leadership must involve steering the group places that such members would not attempt to reach if they were on their own. Attaining this kind of dedication and loyalty is tough without real allegiance motivated by the aspects of true leadership skills. Using rewards, supports, and structure, the leaders encourage effort and reliability. Workers who do their best are rewarded and through reward withholding, those who did not deliver are reproved. The Institution's Management motivates their subordinates to achieve group and organizational goals. The power rests on the employees' and leaders to make sure that they have control over the desired outcomes. For example, it is the duty of a faculty leader to decide how the goals are to be achieved in his department. Effective leadership recognizes high-performing subordinates or those meet their objectives by giving rewards. The programs for encouraging and motivating the staff increase the beliefs in their capacity to achieving set goals and performance. Through positive attitude and aggressiveness expected outcomes are reached. The leaders, besides, identifies efforts and work done by subordinates. If the work done is standard and appealing, then appropriate recommendations are made for promotions (Bryant, 2003).

According to the research, effective leadership and management skills should provide avenues for the association of complementary stimulation and elevation that transforms followers into leaders. Leadership arises when individuals engage in transforming one another. As managers, leaders, and follower interrelate, they build each member to high levels of enthusiasm and standards. A real leadership structure is enhanced through proposed mechanisms that shape, alter, and elevate the motives, ideals, and goals. Through the set policies, followers achieve momentous transformation and progress. The system will acknowledge the existence of an extraordinary strength entangled in modifying leadership principle and support employees. For example, to convert leaders into people who uphold right, desire to achieve, and values, it is advised that the leaders should share freely information with members (Schroeder & Lombardo, 2013). The self-interest of deputies is deemed paramount and transformed into real dreams. Leaders should undertake activities that can increase followers' confidence. Elevated followers' expectations and heightening the value of the leadership create outcomes for the member. Moreover, leaders should encourage behavioral change and motivate others to higher levels of individual accomplishment.

The study concluded that the concept of effective decision-making is a critical tool for organizations to step outside normal patterns of thinking, make innovative solutions, and generate great ideas. Organizations are engaging in complex activities that require critical analysis before execution. When leaders and managers have competencies and experience that can boost the growth of the organization, then they can be applied in the process of making the decision. Leaders should consider brainstorming as a method of generating ideas. Many companies instinctively recognize that they can be performing better when they develop such skills and inculcate them in their organization as the foundation of success. On the other hand, traditional pieces of literature on organization and leadership theory has been dominated nearly entirely by the perception that leadership is something held by just one person. The common principle of team development is essential in solving an existing problem in the enterprise. People outside the organization might influence or be affected by decisions made in an organization. Leaders should learn how to make practical decisions. When leaders are making decisions, they need to have enough information to avoid biases (Bryant, 2003).

Recommendation for Future Research

The research recommends a well-designed investigation to be conducted concerning the effectiveness of supervisory leadership on employees' motivation. There is the need for organizations to understand how leaders can carry out supervision and still motivate employees to work vigorously and be committed to the entire vision (Glatthorn, 1991). Control in an organization means the processes for delivering instruction and guidance, and undertaking monitoring and observation of the employees while performing their respective duties. Control ensures continuity in issuing instruction.

Through the supervisors, all the instructions are communicated to the employee. Supervision provides the control in the organization and the matching of outcomes to plans. Whenever the employees are under constant supervision, deviation from plan is immediately detected and corrective measure employed (Glickman, Gordon, & Ross-Gordon, 2012). When supervisors are engaged in the activities of the organization, resources will be optimally utilized. Workers who are continuously monitored always use the resources in a manner that reduces wastage.

Besides, supervision guarantees discipline within the organization. Under the guidance of a supervisor, the employees will follow a fixed schedule and execute the plans in the right manner. Moreover, the directors are directly involved with the assistants and are the best persons to give feedbacks. The reports regarding the work of every worker used in appraisals should trace back to supervisory activities. The feedback includes information such as complaints, grievances, and problems of employees.

Supervisors issue orders to all the workers and make sure that they are clear, linking the communication gap between the superiors and juniors. Best supervisory practices will improve motivation. A healthy relationship with the supervisor develops the motivation level of the employees encouraging them to perform to their capacity (Komaki & Citera, 1990).

Organizations cannot fully claim total assurance to have found a method of driving consistent performance. Motivating the employees is a persistent challenge requiring adequate attention (Sabanci & Ozdemir, 2015). Bolstering the motivation and practical performance of workers takes time. Therefore, organizations should design and implement plans to motivate workers to sustain productivity. Organizations should make their expectations clear to make the employees aware of the expected goals. The goals should be achievable and measurable, and will become the standards for evaluating their performance. The management should also provide immediately and continuous feedback to the employee to help them know that their actions affect the company.

Employees are motivated when goals are set, and they receive continuous feedback. Employees are encouraged when they discover that they are making progress. It is worth noting that some employees are motivated by negative feedback they receive concerning their performance. Feedback from leaders and managers should involve three main elements: the sources of feedback, the content, and the recipient. Feedback is useful if it is measurable and time bound. The employees and team members are motivated when constant communication culture is created in the organization ensuring that they are informed of their performance, progress, and the changes they need to implement to improve them [productivity and competence. It should be the desire of every manager or leader to raise their effectiveness by incorporating quality feedback to ensure that they inspire progress and save on time. Negative feedback and corrections should be done in private.

The management should consider corrections as a learning opportunity for the employee. Leaders should keep an open mind when correcting their members and recognize that some problems might be outside of an employee's control. Besides, the management should build confidence in their employees. Employers who regularly consider their employees as worthless or underperforming will eventually destroy their emotions (Dunsford, 2003). Employees with damaged emotions will not readily accept to change their behavior or feel the need to improve. Weaknesses of employees should be presented in the way suggesting they can do much better. In transformational leadership, the perception of leaders trust is an essential component.

When employees feel under-appreciated, it encourages complacency. Employees love praise because they thrive on it, and even some are willing to sacrifice incentive and bonuses for public recognition. Organization needs to recognize productive workers and trends within the institution (Shohet, 2000). Leaders should publicly announce instances of employees making a particularly outstanding presentation, large sales, or a notable accomplishment tied with some incentives to accolades, such as bonuses, gifts, or certificates. When the management praises the employees in front of others, then they will be motivated to their continued performance (Schroeder & Lombardo, 2013).

Every organization should consider rewards as a motivational factor for employees. The annual bonus trips are good deals for performing staffs. Although the problem with such rewards is that it leaves the rest of the personal feeling, there is no point in working hard because few people reap the rewards. However, the rewards offer individuals the desire to perform better to be linked to the joy and happiness of receiving similar and better rewards as possible. Setting up series of other smaller rewards throughout the year motivates ongoing performance and excellence. Besides, organizations should vary the basis for the awards to ensure that all employees can achieve the targets and receive the appreciations too. The management should recognize that several types of excellence motivate the employees to focus on additional areas of their performance.

Suggested Questions

Supervisory leadership can affect changes and respectively correct errors in an organization. When associating with the subjects, leaders ought to impart skills and competencies to the employees by being a role model and communicate the important factors that will lead to positive desires to achieve. The structure of the organization, however, determines the extent to which decisive leadership will motivate employees to achieve more effectiveness. The following research questions could lead the recommended study and will assist in determining whether supervision and evaluation could be used to motivate employees (Zepeda, 2001).

Q1:   What is the relationship between supervisory leadership and employee motivation?

Q2:   Can supervisory leadership be used to build the competencies amongst employees?

Q3:   What is the relationship between employee perception on supervisory leadership and personal growth in a competent environment?

Interesting Hypothesis for Future Research

The nature of the organization will determine the results of the recommended research. An Uninformed Organization does not have clear vision or leadership mechanism. The supervisors have no adequate training, and they possess little or no understanding of the pursuit objectives. The supervisors in a Reactive Organization have the tendency of ignoring the incoming change and inputs. They depend upon the behaviors of individuals to make assumptions and predictions. The leaders of a Compliant Organization adhere to the set regulations and are rigid to the extent of securing a compliance culture through training and additional resources (Zepeda, 2001).

Moreover, in a Proactive Organization, the leadership ensures that progress is continuous, and the supervisors will always participate in the activities tailored to initiate commitment and success. Besides, in an Exemplary Organization, the supervisory activities are wholesome and professionally designed. The institution encourages training, communication, motivation, planning, and evaluation of activities on the regular basis to ensure that the rapid progress is occasionally determined. The following hypotheses relate to the questions of the recommended future research (Zepeda, 2001).

H0.1:   There is a significant relationship between supervisory leadership and employee motivation.

H1.1:   There is no significant relationship between supervisory leadership and employee motivation.

H0.2:   Supervisory leadership can be used to build the competencies amongst employees.

H1.2:   Supervisory leadership cannot be used to build the competencies amongst employees.

H0.3: There is a significant relationship between employee perception on

supervisory leadership and personal growth in a competent environment.

H1.3: There is no significant relationship between employee perception on

supervisory leadership and personal growth in a competent environment.

REFERENCES

Bateman, T. S., & Snell, S. (2004). *Managing management: The new competitive landscape* (6th ed.). New York, NY: McGraw-Hill.

Bertocci, D. (2009). Leadership in organizations: There is a difference between leaders and managers. Lanham, MD: United Press of America.

Beveridge, W., (1957). The art of scientistic investigation. New York: Norton.

Bryant, S. E. (2003). The role of transformational and transactional leadership in creating, sharing and exploiting organizational knowledge. *Journal of Leadership and Organizational Studies*, 9(4), 32–44. doi:10.1177/107179190300900403

Charmaz, K. (2006). *Constructing grounded theory.* Belmont, CA: Sage.

Colvard, J. E. (2003). Managers vs. leaders. *Government Executive*, *35*(9), 82–89. Retrieved from http://www.govexec.com/advice-and-comment/viewpoint /2003/07/managers-vs-leaders/14468/

Cooper, D., & Schindler, P. (2014). *Business research methods* (12th ed.) New York, NY: McGraw-Hill.

Cooper, J. (2014). Are you approachable? *Practical Pre-School*, *2014*(164), 19–21. doi:10.12968/prps.2014.1.164.19

Creswell, J. (1998). *Qualitative inquiry and research design: Choosing among five traditions*. Thousand Oaks, CA: Sage.

Denning, Steve. (2014). *The best of Peter Drucker*. Forbes.

DeRue, D. S., & Wellman, N. (2009). Developing leaders via experience: The role of developmental challenge, learning orientation, and feedback availability. *Journal of Applied Psychology*, *94*(4), 859–875. doi:10.1037/a0015317

Drucker, P., (2007). *Management, Edition of management: task, responsibility, practices.* New York: Harper Collins.

Dunsford, H. (2003). *A review of leadership theory and competency frameworks*. Exeter, United Kingdom: Centre for Leadership Studies, University of Exeter.

Edwards, R. S. (2000). *Self-awareness: differences in leaders versus managers in Trinidad and Tobago* (Doctoral dissertation). Available from ProQuest Dissertations & Theses database. (UMI No. 304622820).

Fiedler, F. E. (1996). Research on leadership selection and training: One view of the future. *Administrative Science Quarterly*, *41*(2), 241–250. doi:10.2307/2393716

Fred Garcia, H. (2006). Effective leadership response to crisis. *Strategy & Leadership, 34*(1), 4–10. doi:10.1108/10878570610637849

Ganesan, S. (2010). Effective leadership: My view. *Asia-Pacific Psychiatry, 2*(4), 175–175. doi:10.1111/j.1758-5872.2010.00086.x

George, J., & Gereth, J. (2005). *Understanding and managing organizational behavior* (4th ed.). Boston, MA: Prentice Hall.

Gibson, J. L., Ivancevich, J. M., & Donnelly, J. H. (2000). *Organizations: Behavior, structure, processes* (10th ed.). Boston, MA: McGraw-Hill.

Glaser, B. (1978). *Constructivist grounded theory.* Beverly Hills, CA: Sage.

Glaser, B., & Strauss, A. (1967). *The discovery of grounded theory: Strategies for qualitative research.* Chicago, IL: Aldine.

Glatthorn, A. A. (1991). Supervisory leadership: Introduction to Instructional Supervision. *NASSP Bulletin, 75*(533), 119–120. doi:10.1177/019263659107553324

Glickman, C. D., Gordon, S. P., & Ross-Gordon, J. M. (2012). *The basic guide to supervision and instructional leadership* (3rd ed.). Boston, MA: Allyn & Bacon.

Hersey, P. & Blanchard, K. H. (1996). Great ideas revisited: Revisiting the life-cycle theory of leadership. *Training and Development, 50*(1), 42–47.

Ingram, D. (2014). *The importance of leadership in business.* Retrieved from http://smallbusiness.chron.com/importance-leadership-business-3117.html

Ivonne, P. (2010). *Professionalization, leadership and management in the early years.* London, England: Sage.

Johnson, C. E. (2009). *Meeting the ethical challenges for leadership: Casting light or shadow.* Thousand Oaks, CA: Sage.

Kim, S.-I., Shin, S. I., & Du, K. H. (2014). The qualitative study on the process of leadership flexibility based on organizational leaders schemas. *Korean Journal of Counseling, 15*(2), 987–1008. doi:10.15703/kjc.15.2.201404.987

Komaki, J. L., & Citera, M. (1990). Beyond effective supervision: Identifying key interactions between superior and subordinate. *Leadership Quarterly, 1*(2), 91–105. doi:10.1016/1048-9843(90)90008-6

Kotter, J. P. (1996). *Leading change.* Brighton, MA. Harvard Business School Press.

Kotter, J. P. (2009). *What leaders really do*. Brighton, MA. Harvard Business School Press

Krasman, J. (2009). The feedback-seeking personality: Big Five and feedback-seeking behavior. *Journal of Leadership and Organizational Studies*, *17*(1), 18–32. doi:10.1177/1548051809350895

Leadership vs management: What's the difference? (2001). *Healthcare Executive*, *16*(6), 26.

Leedy, P.D., & Ormond, J. E. (2010). Practical Research: Planning and Design. (9th ed.) NYC: Merrill.

Lewin, K., Lippit, R., & White, R. K. (1939). Patterns of aggressive behavior in experimentally created social climates. *Journal of Social Psychology*, *10*, 271–301.

Lopez, R. (2014). The relationship between leadership and management: Instructional approaches and its connections to organizational growth. *Journal of Business Studies Quarterly*, *6*(1), 98–112. Retrieved from http://jbsq.org/wp-content/uploads/2014/09/September_2014_7.pdf

Mann, S. (2006). Leadership training. *Leadership and Organization Development Journal*, *27*(7). doi:10.1108/lodj.2006.02227gae.004

Mendez-Morse, S. (2004). Constructing mentors: Latina educational leaders role models and mentors. *Educational Administration Quarterly*, *40*(4), 561–590. doi:10.1177/0013161x04267112

Mitut, I. (2011). The role of leadership in the management of crisis situations. *Romanian Economic and Business Review*, *6*(3), 20–33. Retrieved from https://ideas.repec.org/a/rau/journl/v6y2011i3p20-33.html

Moustakas, C. (1994). *Phenomenological research methods*. Belmont, CA: Sage.

Murray, A.. (2010). *The wall street journal essential guide to management: lasting lessons from the best leadership minds of our time*. New York City, NY: Harper Publishing.

Needed: Transformational leaders. (2002). *BMJ*, *325*(7376). doi:10.1136/bmj.325.7376.0/e

Nienaber, H. (2010). Conceptualisation of management and leadership. *Management Decision*, *48*(5), 661–675. doi:10.1108/00251741011043867

Northouse, P. G. (2009). *Introduction to leadership: Concepts and practice.* Thousand Oaks, CA: Sage.

Organizational structure. (n.d.). *Oxford Dictionaries Online.* Retrieved September 26, 2015, from http://www.oxforddictionaries.com/us/spellcheck/american_english /?q=organizational+structure

Oxford University Press. (2016). http://www.oxforddictionaries.com/definition/english/administrator?q=Administr ator

Padgett, K. (2004). *The qualitative research experience.* Belmont, CA: Wadsworth.

Parisian, D. (2009). *Training managers to become change leaders* (Doctoral dissertation). Available from ProQuest Dissertations & Theses Database. (UMI No. 894268773).

Patton, M. (1980). *Qualitative evaluation methods.* Beverly Hills, CA: Sage.

Poletiek, F. H. (2013). *Hypothesis-testing behavior.* Philadelphia, PA: Psychology Press.

Potts, J. D. (2001). *The ethical difference: Why leaders are more than managers.* Longmont, CO: Rocky Mountain Press.

Proctor, T. (2003). *Essentials of marketing research.* (3rd ed.) Prentise Hall. Pg.100.

Pugh,, D. S., (1990). *Organization theory: selected readings.* Harmondsworth: Penguin.

Relevant development: Effective leadership training. (2012). *Development and Learning in Organizations, 26*(5), 32–36. doi:10.1108/14777281211258699

Richards, L. (2014). *Business leadership issues.* Retrieved from http://smallbusiness .chron.com/business-leadership-issues–2978.html

Richardson, J. M. (2007). *Leaders vs. managers: It is not what you think* (Doctoral dissertation). Available from ProQuest Dissertations & Theses database. (UMI No. 304707278).

Rubin, A., & Babbie, E. (2001). *Research methods for social work.* Belmont, CA: Wadsworth.

Sabanci, A., & Ozdemir, I. (2015). Team leadership: Leadership role achievement in supervision teams in Turkey. *International Journal of Academic Research in Business and Social Sciences, 5*(3). 243–260. doi:10.6007/ijarbss/v5-i3/1521

Sanford, K. D. (2011). How to fill key leadership positions strategically. *Healthcare Financial Management, 65*(6), 44–48. Retrieved from http://www.ncbi.nlm.nih .gov/pubmed/21692375

Schettler, J. (2002). Leadership in corporate America. *Training, 39*(9), 66–77. Retrieved from http://www.ccl.org/leadership/pdf/news/releases/trainingmagazine.pdf

Schroeder, D., & Lombardo, F. (2013). *Management and supervision of law enforcement personnel* (5th ed.). Charlottesville, VA: LexisNeixs.

Seabury, C. (2014). What are leadership skills in big business? Retrieved from http://smallbusiness.chron.com/leadership-skills-big-business-43384.html

Shohet, R. (2000). *Supervision in the helping professions: And individual, group and organizational approach* (2nd ed.). Philadelphia, PA: Open University Press.

Sinclair, A., & Sinclair, A. (2004). *Doing leadership differently: Gender, power, and sexuality in a changing business culture*. Victoria, Australia: Melbourne University Press.

Strauss, A., & Corbin, J. (1990). *Basics of qualitative research: Grounded theory procedures and techniques*. Newbury Park, CA: Sage.

Stoghill, R. M. (1974). *Handbook of leadership: A survey of theory and research*. New York, NY: Free Press.

Sullivan, E. J. (2012). *Effective leadership and management in nursing: International edition* (8th ed.). Boston: Pearson.

Sutton, T. E. (2006). *Managers, reform and leadership: Making managers leaders* (Doctoral dissertation). Available from ProQuest Dissertations & Theses database. (UMI No. 304962036).

Sweeney, P. (2001). What's the difference between leaders and managers? *Franchising World, 33*(4), 64–65. Retrieved from http://connection.ebscohost.com/c/articles /4704947/whats-difference-between-leaders-managers

Toyota. (2015). Vision and mission statement. Retrieved from http://toyota.custhelp.com /app/answers/detail/a_id/7654/~/what-are-toyotas-mission-and-vision-statements %3F

Watson, G., & Reissner, S. C. (2010). *Developing skills for business leadership*. London, England: Chartered Institute of Personnel and Development.

Weathersby, G. B. (1999). Leadership vs. management. *Management Review, 88*(3), 5. Retrieved from http://search.proquest.com/openview/218e7e5ff73dea92fedf831 bdee40c04/1?pq-origsite=gscholar

Welch, J. (2005). *Winning.* New York: Harper Collins.

Weyer, M. V. (2011, September 3). Steve Jobs: The perfectionist who raised industrial design to the level of high art. *The Spectator*. Retrieved from http://www.spectator.co.uk/2011/09/any-other-business-56/

Wiesner, P. (1997). Leadership or management? *Colorado Business Magazine, 24*(6), 9.

Wilcox, R. R. (2012). *Introduction to robust estimation and hypothesis testing.* San Diego, CA: Academic Press.

William, M. M. W. (2011). *Advances in global leadership* (Illustrated ed.). Bingley, England: Emerald.

Wilson, J. (1997). Building the vision: Lessons for all leaders. *Computer, 30*(11), 135–136. doi:10.1109/mc.1997.634869

Zaleznik, A. (1977, May–June). Managers and leaders: Are they different? *Harvard Business Review*. Retrieved from https://hbr.org/2004/01/managers-and-leaders -are-they-different

Zaleznik, A. (1992, March–April). Managers and leaders: Are they different? *Harvard Business Review*, 126–135.

Zepeda, S. J. (2001). At odds: Can supervision and evaluation co-exist? *Journal of Cases in Educational Leadership, 4*(1), 1–22. doi:10.1177/155545890100400101

www.ingramcontent.com/pod-product-compliance
Lightning Source LLC
Chambersburg PA
CBHW081740220526

45468CB00008B/2172

* 9 7 8 1 9 8 3 8 4 8 4 3 8 *